Love Stories from the Quran

ISBN: 978-967-2420-26-2
First Edition: June 2019
Second Edition: June 2020

For inquiry, please contact:

Tertib Publishing
23-2 Jalan PJS 5/30
Petaling Jaya Commercial City (PJCC)
46150 Petaling Jaya, Selangor
Malaysia
Tel: +603-7772-3156 / +6013-399-8837
Email: info@tertib.press

Website: www.tertib.press

Cover design: Miza Mumtaz
Editor: Dahlia Abdul Latiff
Typesetting & Layout: Ainul Syuhada
Printed by: Firdaus Press Sdn. Bhd.

Contents

Preface

With the Name of Allah and after the choicest benedictions and salutations upon the final Messenger of Allah - Muhammed Sala Allahu alihi wasSalaam.

The Qur'ān is not a storybook of wondrous tales and ancient fables, isolated from the realities and complexities of real life. Each verse, in fact, each letter is miraculously precise in meaning, succinct in message and pure in sound.

'Ali radyAllāhu 'anhu came home one day from a journey that he had been dispatched on by the Prophet Muhammed sallallāhu 'alayhi wa sallam, to find his wife, Fatima, the daughter of the Prophet, radiya Allahu 'anha brushing her teeth with a siwak – twig of an Arak (Salvadora persica) tree used for brushing teeth. Spontaneously, he, radyAllāhu 'anhu, spouted out poetic endearment:

هنئت يا عود الأراك بثغرها ... أما خشيت يا أراكُ أراك

لو كان غيرك يا سواك قتلته ... ما فاز مني يا سواكُ سواك

Fortunate are you O twig of the Arak tree,

Have you no fear of me observing you in this embrace

If it were other than you…O Siwak! I would have killed you!

None found this fortune of embrace before me, but you..

Love. The real kind – the genuine love between a man and his wife that stems from a seed of love that is planted by Allah in the hearts of those who are true in submission to the Dispenser of Love and Comfort.

A seed, literally and figuratively, in Arabic symbolizes love.

Houb in Arabic is derived from the same root for the word Haab – seed. The nature of the two words is functionally similar.

Love begins as a tiny speck – a seed that is buried deep in the folds of a receptive heart, carrying the potential of stunning beauty, nourishing sustenance, exotic delicacy, wealth of commodity, shading shelter, and resurgent growth that is stabilized through deep roots that withstand trauma.

The aim of this book is to connect us to the Quran and to Allah by extension of Love.

The Quran is Arabic. Translations are the work of beings seeking to comprehend and render in their own words a description of what that Word means to them. The beauty of the Quran is multidimensional and inimitable.

It is important to note that many Quranic verses establish men and women inclusively in the broad terms of "human being" or "people" (insan, nas). Although these words are masculine pronouns in Arabic, and translate to "man," "mankind," or "men," they are gender-neutral in the original Arabic and apply to women as much as they do to men.

It is important to also keep in mind that when a group includes both Muslim men and Muslim women they are referred to with the male form collective noun muslimun. In most cases it refers to all Muslims, irrespective of gender.

This is an important clarification for those who can only access the Quran as a translation or are confronted with a male centric English translation that does not reflect the reality of the Quran in its original Arabic. Where the Quran mentions men and women separately, it is clear and unambiguous.

The Quran's basic stance is that Muslim men are the religious equals of Muslim women. They assist and protect one another:

Anyone, male or female, who does good deeds and is a believer, will enter Paradise and will not be wronged by as much as the dip in a date stone. (Quran: 4:124)

The believers, both men and women, support each

other; they order what is right and forbid what is wrong; they keep up the prayer and pay the prescribed alms; they obey God and His Messenger. God will give His mercy to such people: God is almighty and wise. (Quran 9:71)

The Quran describes the Muslim marriage in terms of love and mercy interchanged between two separate but equal parts that come into one another:

It is He who created you all from one soul, and from it made its mate so that he might find comfort in her: when one [of them] lies with his wife and she conceives a light burden, going about freely, then grows heavy, they both pray to God, their Lord, 'If You give us a good child we shall certainly be grateful,' (Quran 7:189)

Another of His signs is that He created spouses from among yourselves for you to live with in tranquillity: He ordained love and kindness between you. There truly are signs in this for those who reflect. (Quran 30:21)

A pray that these words build love for us and between us and make us true in our love.

In need of your sincere dua,

Yahya Adel Ibrahim

Perth, Western Australia

Love Stories from the
Quran

Stories

We often associate stories with fables, legends, and myths. They are bedtime stories and passing anecdotes. Few would care to examine them with depth and clarity; most people only read them with a surface level of understanding. But Allah (s.w.t.) uses stories to tell original accounts of the human experience. By providing a narrative that can be felt to the depth of our own failure and depression, sadness and loss, and comfort and happiness, He creates a guiding compass for our lives. We find this compass in the stories of others whose fates He has divulged to us, studying and living it with them. It is in this way that we can find ourselves in those accounts of people long gone, whether they were better or worse than we are.

Upon opening the Qur'an, Allah (s.w.t.) invites us to see the parable or metaphor for every position we may find ourselves in over the course of our lives. Every struggle has been addressed in the Qur'an. A single mother finds herself in Maryam (a.s.). A single father who worries about his daughters finds himself in Lut (a.s.). A good man with a wayward son or a misguided wife finds himself in Nuh (a.s.) and Lut (a.s.). A good woman enduring life with a tyrant husband, with the belief that she can have a house in paradise, finds herself in Asiya, the wife of Fir'awn.

A young man who sees his father as overbearing and difficult can empathise with the issues Ibrahim (a.s.) had with his only father figure. When one's own flesh and blood conspires against them, seeks to harm them, and backbites about them, holding murderous intentions if they only had the chance, the story of Yusuf (a.s.) is a source of comfort.

On the other hand, a man with a loving brother who carries him in high esteem, lifts his spirit, and elevates him to a better place, is like Harun (a.s.) with his brother Musa (a.s.). A wonderful father with an obedient son, who walks in his step hand in hand, treading along paths with his father, finds himself close to Ibrahim (a.s.), Ishaq (a.s.), and Ismail (a.s.).

These are not invented stories. These are *qasas*—narratives. Out of the 124,000 prophets sent to humanity, as mentioned in a *hadith* (the tradition or saying of Prophet Muhammad [s.a.w.]) recorded by Imam Ahmad, only 25 prophets are mentioned to us in the Qur'an and the Sunnah. They were the only ones whose lives were detailed for us because they encapsulate the messages of the unnamed, whose lives and deeds are known only to Allah (s.w.t.). The fact that only stories about these 25 prophets were revealed proves that it is especially important for us to pay attention and study the messages and lessons embodied in them.

The main goal of the Qur'an is to acquaint mankind with Allah (s.w.t.). It is a manual sent to teach us how we must live in connection with Him, rather than with this world.

Love

Love is powerful. Love can inspire one to sacrifice or pursue adventure, and it can send one to the road of happiness or the road of sorrow. Love can be blind, and it can be destructive. All of these effects of love are discussed in the Qur'an, in narratives gifted to us by Allah (s.w.t.).

The concept of the word for love in Arabic, "*hubb*", comes from the purity of teeth. When someone's teeth are beaming white and their cleanliness is visible, it could be said that they are pure and unadulterated. That is how the Arabs would define love.

The idea of worship in Islam is often misunderstood by Muslims themselves. The words *'ibadah* (worship) and *'ubudiyyah* (servitude) signify the height of love. One's relationship with Allah (s.w.t.) and one's *tawhid* (attributing Oneness to Allah) start with *ilm* (knowledge).

Ilm on its own, however, is ineffective. It must transcend in the second stage into certainty: a conviction that is not based on fragile ideas taken from a religious text, *hadith*, or conversation, but a conviction that comes from genuine faith.

The third stage is when certainty transforms into acceptance. What Allah (s.w.t.) says, we accept. The commands we are given may sometimes be difficult to fulfil, but it is from the One Who knows it is better for us, even if we do not understand it. A command from Allah (s.w.t.), therefore, will not be rejected.

Acceptance is followed by submission, which is a different type of struggle. The level of submission to Allah's wills and commands is a gauge for how strong one's *tawhid* is.

Next comes *sidq*: being true to Allah (s.w.t.).

Once, a sister approached me to express a concern. *Shaykh, I have been married for a few months now, and I have a problem: I married a fajr-beard.*

What is a fajr-beard? This is a new term for me.

She replied, *When a brother has a long beard that tells you he prays fajr. But I married a bearded man that doesn't pray fajr. What do I do?*

So I said, *Inna lillahi wa inna ilayhi raji'un.*

Some of us hope that our children fulfil their *salah* (prayer) right when we order them, but in truth, we are using an ineffective parenting strategy. Instead of inviting our children to join us in prayer, we command them to go and pray; so they have not been raised with the practice of building the family routine around gathering in prayer at its appointed times. Allah (s.w.t) says,

وَأْمُرْ أَهْلَكَ بِالصَّلَاةِ وَاصْطَبِرْ عَلَيْهَا...

And enjoin prayer upon your family [and people] and be steadfast therein...
(Surah Taha, 20:132)

Sidq eventually leads to *ikhlas*: sincerity. *Ikhlas* is often mentioned in lectures and *khutbahs* (sermons). But it is not the beginning of our relationship with Allah (s.w.t.); it is the completion of it.

After *ikhlas*, one ascends to *al-mahabbah* or *hubb.* It is out of the love for Allah (s.w.t.) that everything we received and everything we do draw us closer to Him, Al-Wadud (The Loving). Those who believe, do righteous deeds, and are consistent in their faith and their application of it, The Ever Merciful shall establish for them love among mankind to them and love between them and Allah (s.w.t.). This is true love, not a misguiding infatuation. In future chapters, we will learn about the examples from the Qur'an of the difference between the true love that brings us closer to Allah (s.w.t.) and the false love that leads us away from Him.

Al-Quran

The Qur'an was sent to Muhammad (s.a.w.) in a unique way. From the time of Adam (a.s.) to the time of 'Isa (a.s.), for thousands of years, there was always a prophet and a messenger who walked the earth calling people to the truth. They had a link to The Creator, and an angel would visit them with the delivery of divine scriptures, and they would notify people of the ordainments of Allah (s.w.t.).

As a mark of the seal of prophethood, Muhammad (s.a.w.) was not sent with another prophet to assist him, as was the case with all others. Musa (a.s.), Harun (a.s.), and Yusha' (a.s.) were sent together; Ibrahim (a.s.), Lut (a.s.), Ishaq (a.s.), and Isma'il (a.s.) were sent together; Zakariyya (a.s.), Yahya (a.s.), and 'Isa (a.s.) were sent together. But after 'Isa (a.s.), for 600 years, the earth grew dark. The revelation was held back. No communication from heaven descended upon mankind.

In *Sahih Al-Bukhari*, the Prophet (s.a.w.) said that between him and 'Isa (a.s.), there were no prophets and messengers—there was darkness. And then he came like daybreak. He was like the light of the moon in the night, bringing with him guidance and clarity. People would gravitate to him, not for who he was, but for what he delivered. The Qur'an was unlike the scriptures before it, because Muhammad (s.a.w.) needed no help from anyone to bear the burden with him.

When given the message, Musa (a.s.) requested, *O Allah, send me someone to carry this burden with me, someone from my family, my brother, Harun.*

What Musa (a.s.) asked for was provided to the Prophet Muhammad (s.a.w.) without him seeking for it. In the Qur'an, Allah (s.w.t.) mentions that He Himself carries the burden and makes it lighter on the Prophet (s.a.w.).

Did We not expand for you, [O Muhammad], your breast? And We removed from you your burden, which had weighed upon your back.
(Surah Al-Inshirah, 94:1–3)

The Qur'an was sent as the completion and as a renewal of the scriptures of that had been changed by those who came before us. It fills in gaps and corrects corrupted narratives. In this book, we will clarify some of these gaps and corruptions that may have been overlooked or misunderstood by us Muslims.

The First Love Story
Adam (a.s.) & Hawwa

We begin our journey with Adam (a.s.). When he was created, our souls were created with his. As mentioned in one narration, Adam (a.s.) was admitted to *Jannah (Paradise)*, and he asked for a companion, someone from his own soul, from himself, created by Allah (s.w.t.) for his comfort and happiness. Human beings are not meant to live without such bond and affinity to one another—to a person who completes them. Even an eternity of bliss in *Jannah* itself is not whole without someone to enjoy it with. And we take this understanding from the Prophet (s.a.w.).

One of the promises given to us by Allah (s.w.t.) in the Qur'an is that when we return to Him, He joins us with those who had passed away before us in this life. When we are in the next life, we receive news of those we leave behind in the *dunya* (this world), and we will wait in anticipation for them to join us in the *akhirah* (the afterlife). That is why when we visit the graveyard, we say, *Asalamu'alaykum, O people in the graves, O people of homes. You have reached the destination before us. We will catch up with you shortly, insha'Allah.*

In his final moments, Prophet Muhammad (s.a.w.) had an affectionate exchange with his daughter, Fatimah (r.a.), as narrated by 'A'ishah (r.a.):

دَعَا النَّبِيُّ صلى الله عليه وسلم فَاطِمَةَ ابْنَتَهُ فِي شَكْوَاهُ الَّذِي قُبِضَ فِيهَا، فَسَارَّهَا بِشَىْءٍ فَبَكَتْ، ثُمَّ دَعَاهَا فَسَارَّهَا فَضَحِكَتْ، قَالَتْ فَسَأَلْتُهَا عَنْ ذَلِكَ. فَقَالَتْ سَارَّنِي النَّبِيُّ صلى الله عليه وسلم فَأَخْبَرَنِي أَنَّهُ يُقْبَضُ فِي وَجَعِهِ الَّذِي تُوُفِّيَ فِيهِ فَبَكَيْتُ، ثُمَّ سَارَّنِي فَأَخْبَرَنِي أَنِّي أَوَّلُ أَهْلِ بَيْتِهِ أَتْبَعُهُ فَضَحِكْتُ

The Prophet (s.a.w.) called his daughter Fatimah during his illness in which he died and told her a secret, whereupon she wept. Then he called her again and told her a secret, whereupon she laughed. When I asked her about that, she replied, "The Prophet (s.a.w.) spoke to me in secret and informed me that he would die in the course of the illness during which he died, so I wept. He again spoke to me in secret and informed

me that I would be the first of his family to follow him [after his death] and on that, I laughed."
(*Sahih Al-Bukhari*)

Fatimah (r.a.) was happy to hear about dying right after him because she knew that the moment she would pass on, the person to greet her and meet her would be her own father and Prophet, Muhammad (s.a.w.).

When Bilal (r.a.) was on his deathbed, his wife exclaimed in poetry, *O my sorrow. O my devastation at these moments of you leaving me.*

He responded, *Silence. O what a joyous day it is! Today I meet Muhammad and his companions.*

Jannah is not enough on its own. Adam (a.s.) and his wife lived in *Jannah* in happiness. They were commanded not to come near, touch, or eat from the forbidden tree; and it was just one tree out of all the endless trees in *Jannah*. Adam (a.s.) forgot, and when the shaytan whispered to them, they ate from the tree. They were sent out of *Jannah* and brought down to the earth on different parts of the world. Some would say that Jeddah (which means "grandparent" in the Arabic language) is named like it is because it is where she descended. In one of the narrations shared with us is that on a sacred day (which we still hold as being the most sacred day of the year),

Adam (a.s.) wondered throughout the earth, looking for his beloved. The one whom he loved in *Jannah*, he wished to love and embrace in the *dunya*. So he roamed the earth, searching for her. He climbed up a small mountain, and a little bit after the time of *'asr* and before the time of *maghrib*, from a distance, he saw Hawwa. He descended from the mountain and embrace her when they were finally reunited. They said,

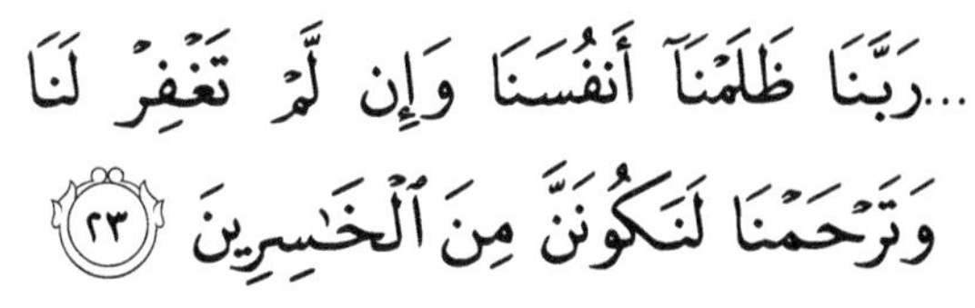

...Our Lord, we have wronged ourselves.
And if You do not forgive us and grant us
Your mercy, then we will remain as losers.
(Surah Al-A'raf, 7:23)

That day became the Day of 'Arafah, the Day of Recognition: the recognition of our obligation to Allah (s.w.t.) and the recognition of the importance of families in our life.

They walked from that sacred moment. That was the first time human beings petitioned together on earth, asking for forgiveness. So, we recreate that day. When we go for *hajj* (pilgrimage), we remember the love story that precedes it—a love story that began in heaven and came to the Earth. They walked until they came to a valley that was marked for them by Jibril (a.s.). That spot was where they first did their *salah*. The first time and the first place human beings put their forehead to the ground in servitude to Allah (s.w.t.) was there. So erected around it was a perimeter that we refer to as the Ka'bah. Its sacredness is in the rocks that it is built with, which were chipped and broken with time, then rebuilt generation after generation. Its sacredness is in that it is the spot that our father and mother—out of love for each other and for Allah (s.w.t.)—submitted themselves to Him. The first dedicated house of worship of mankind is in that valley of Makkah Al-Mukarramah. It is a place of sanctity and *barakah* (blessing).

This is the story of Adam (a.s.) and Hawwa—a love story that is mentioned to us in the Qur'an.

The Lessons

1st *Lesson*

It is important that we generate a spirit of connection and harmony with our spouses and in our home life. Adam (a.s.) traversed the earth looking for his wife Hawwa; he did not ask Allah (s.w.t.) to replace her. In fact, his love for her was beautiful and can be clearly seen through his actions—she was from him, a part of him, and he would not give up on finding her even if it meant scaling the earth.

2nd Lesson

Adam (a.s.) and Hawwa, our ancestral parents, endured difficulty. It is painful to imagine being in *Jannah* and having a simple limit set to oneself yet still fail to adhere to it. The Prophet (s.a.w.) narrated the interchange between Musa (a.s.) and Adam (a.s.), as reported in *Sahih Al-Bukhari*. After Musa (a.s.) died, he met Adam (a.s.) and was upset.

Musa (a.s.) said, *Allah created you with His own hand and made everything subservient to you and the angels prostrated to you. He entered you into Jannah, created for you a spouse, gave you everything you wanted. He ordered you not to eat from just one tree, yet you still went and ate from it. What is wrong with you?*

Adam (a.s.) responded, *Do you blame me for something that was written for me 50,000 years before I was made? Allah created me with this defect, knowing that I have the capacity to forget. Do I need to remind you, O Musa, that Allah told you not to kill anyone?*

Thus, Adam (a.s.) defeated Musa (a.s.) in their argument. That is how a father usually responds—you do not embarrass your son. Adam (a.s.) did not say, *Hey, why are you talking to me about a tree? What about your mistake?* Rather, he reminded him that his flaws were written for him and that Musa (a.s.) himself had forgotten something even greater.

It does not matter what you have experienced in life or how much faith you have today; they do not necessarily guarantee that you will successfully pass the tests to come, which you are not aware of yet. Allah (s.w.t.) does not expect us to not make any mistakes at all. Instead, He wants us to return to Him every time we fall into sin.

Walk the earth until you find someone who will remind you to say,

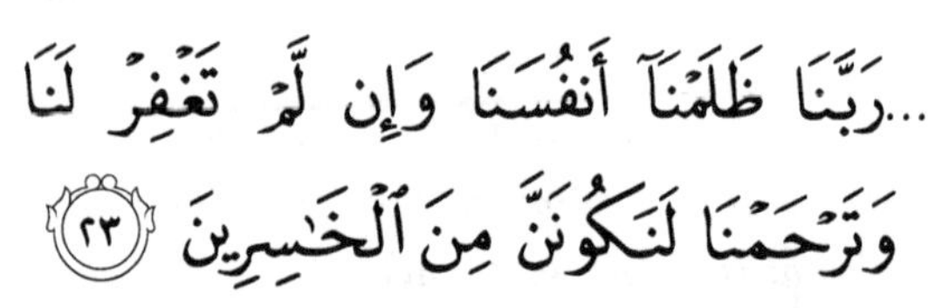

...Our Lord, we have wronged ourselves.
And if You do not forgive us and grant us
Your mercy, then we will remain as losers.
(Surah Al-A'raf, 7:23)

Love & Beautiful Patience
Yusuf (a.s.)

We have just spoken about true love: the love created by Allah (s.w.t.) between a husband and his wife, Adam (a.s.) and Hawwa. Now let's speak about what masquerades as love: what looks, feels, and sounds like love but, in reality, is foreign to it.

Every *surah* (chapter) in the Qur'an has an underlying theme: the clear message of the *surah*. The theme of Surah Yusuf is love. It is the love of a father for his son. It is the love of a son for his father. It is the false love, the infatuation, the sinful and passionate lust of a woman for a man. It is the love of the *dunya* where people would kidnap a son, or brothers would conspire against one of their own. It is the love of authority and kingdom. Love of all shapes and shades are discussed in Surah Yusuf.

However, we are going to focus on just two aspects of it. The first aspect is *ishq* (passion). Imam Ibn Al-Qayyim speaks about love being of two types:

1 | True love that is pleasing to Allah (s.w.t.)

It is the exchange of love between one another that is not an act of sin. For example, the love of a husband for his wife, a father and a mother for their children, and the children for their parents and grandparents. This type of love is blessed and honourable—it is pleasing to Allah (s.w.t.).

In fact, the Prophet (s.a.w.) said that we should not separate two people who love one another. In an authentic *hadith*, a man came to the Prophet (s.a.w.) and said, *O Messenger of Allah, I have been raising a young girl who was an orphan from the moment she was born, and I have been like her father. She is old enough to be married now, and two men have come to ask for her hand. One of them is a respectable man and a believer who has wealth and holds status. The other is a believer and a good man, but he is poor. She loves the poor man but does not like the rich man. I have been her caregiver, and I want the best for her. Both of them are good people, but one of them has something that the other lacks. What do you think I should do, o Messenger of Allah?*

In this kind of circumstance, the Prophet (s.a.w.) would never say, *Do this*, or *Do that*. Because when the matters of the heart were involved, it was not for him to make that determination unless *wahy* (revelation from Allah) was sent down with specific instructions. So instead, the Prophet (s.a.w.) simply said, *In my opinion, never separate between two people who love each other.*

It is an important moment where the hearts connect. Perhaps that man who was wealthy could have his wealth taken by Allah (s.w.t.), and perhaps that man who was poor could become wealthy by Allah (s.w.t.) increasing his provision.

In another *hadith* in *Sahih Muslim*, Prophet Muhammad (s.a.w.) was sitting with the *sahabah* (companions) when a man walked by. The Prophet (s.a.w.) whispered to them, *What do you think of this man who has just walked by?*

They replied, *O Messenger of Allah, he is the best of us! He is the best to his family. He is a wealthy man. If he gives me advice, I will listen. If he speaks on behalf of someone, I will listen to his speech. If he asks for someone in my family to marry him, I would be honoured.*

The Prophet (s.a.w.) was quiet. Another man walked by later on, and the Prophet inquired again, *What do you think of this one?*

They responded, *O Messenger of Allah, he is not of the best of us. He is not wealthy. If he gives me advice, I will go against him. If he speaks on behalf of someone, I will go against them as well. If he asks for someone from my family, I would be insulted.*

The Prophet (s.a.w.) said, *This one that you speak critically of—one of him with Allah is better than the whole earth populated by the first one you spoke highly of.*

Sometimes we judge by the wrong scales.

2 | *Masquerading love*

It is a sinful love: an infatuation or impassioned love that is built on the same emotions and the same feelings but causes you to sin to reach it. It feels the same as the first love mentioned above, and the people involved want the same experiences. Everything that describes true love is found in it. But to get it, sin must be committed. That is called *ishq*. The man or woman compromises their relationship with Allah (s.w.t.) to achieve something that He created and that He can give it to them without such a sacrifice. Allah (s.w.t.) will give love in the right way, to the right person, at the right time.

In that sense, *ishq* is that wayward text message, that secret meeting, that promise, or that look that one would hate for any human being, let alone his or her family, to know what they were doing. This is not the kind of love praised by Allah (s.w.t.), and it is sinful.

Such is the example of that "love" offered to Yusuf (a.s.). The wife of his master attempted to entice him like any seductress would approach a man in such a circumstance, but he refused, saying, *I seek refuge in Allah*—because his heart had an inkling towards it. How could he not be enticed by the offer? She sought him, and he could have accepted her. Had his Lord, Allah, not saved him with clear evidence of its sinfulness and immorality, he would have felt comfortable in fulfiling such a desire. But he was a sincere servant of Allah (s.w.t.), and Allah (s.w.t.) made his heart firm. When one is truthful and sincere, Allah (s.w.t.) helps him in times when he cannot help himself.

So the next time, she locked everything up and kicked all the other servants out, saying, *I have made everything ready. There is no escape today.* Yet he still ran.

The *'ulama* (scholars) commented on why Yusuf (a.s.) ran towards the door despite the fact that he knew it was locked: it was because he needed to escape from her. She grabbed him and scratched him, and as she pulled him by the back of his shirt, it ripped!

His master—her husband—returned. He was at the door. He understood the reality of his situation. What we do not realise about the story of Yusuf (a.s.) is that the one who began the pattern of dishonesty was the master himself, as he said to his wife, *Maybe we can claim him as our son*, when Yusuf (a.s.) was found in the well.

When he arrived, she declared, *What are you going to do with a man who assaults your wife?*

Yusuf (a.s.) said, *Look, it is she who chased me, and the people are witnesses.*

All the evidence was there. Finally, the master said to his wife, *You have wronged yourself; your evil has shown itself*, and he said to Yusuf (a.s.), *Forget about this.*

The people in the city begin to mock her. The women in the village said she became so insane and impassioned with this infatuation that it penetrated all aspects of decency. She did not care about her self-respect when he did not want to be with her. She did not care about his age, what her husband would think, what his or her family would think, or what society would say. She lost her entire reputation—for a servant.

The promise of the Prophet (s.a.w.) is true. Those who commit sexual misconduct and immorality should know with certainty that their deed would be exposed in the midst of their home. Allah (s.w.t.) will reveal it to those in their own home, the ones whom they would hate them to know about the sin. It is the one deed in which the punishment in this life is humiliating exposure.

Yusuf (a.s.) was further mistreated with imprisonment. Until one day, the king of Egypt had a strange dream—no one could interpret it but Yusuf (a.s.). So the king sent for him. Yusuf (a.s.) said, *Ask about what really happened to the women who cut their hands.*

He wanted them to know the truth. The women replied that they knew nothing wrong about Yusuf (a.s.). In the end, the wife of his former master admitted that she was the one at fault and that she wished to repent. Some books of *tafsir* (translation and interpretation of the Qur'an) mention that after the death of her husband, she married Yusuf (a.s.).

Through this story, we learn about true love and redemption. Because of his true love for Allah (s.w.t.) and his patience with Allah (s.w.t.), everything that was taken away from him by others was returned to him by Allah (s.w.t.). Yusuf (a.s.) was rewarded with a position in the kingdom. His brothers who threw him into the well were sent to him in their time of need. He recognised them, but they did not. At this point, they were at this mercy—the food was in his hand. He saved his brothers, and he taught them forgiveness and compassion.

It was a redemption where things came to full circle. His father's eyesight that was gone because of him missing the scent and the embrace of his son, by the will of Allah (s.w.t.), returned to him just by smelling Yusuf's shirt. And Yusuf (a.s.) was finally reunited with his father and mother.

The Lessons

1st *Lesson*

Harm is inescapable. There will be people who are supposed to care for you, but they will not. There will be people who will steal from you. There will be people who harbour jealousy or ill feelings towards you—even among your own flesh and blood. There are examples in the Qur'an.

2nd Lesson

Never do to others as they have done to you in a sinful way. Never take revenge on abuse. What elevated Yusuf (a.s.) status—from being a slave to having the kingdom of Egypt in the palm of his hand—was his patience. Allah (s.w.t.) mentions patience twice in the *surah*:

...فَصَبْرٌ جَمِيلٌ...

...So [I can only endure with] beautiful patience...

The beauty is in patience. Do not respond to cruelty with cruelty—if you do so, you will only be equal to the wrongdoers, and you will be punished similarly. The punishment is that you will be left to your own devices, without any divine assistance. However, if you endure with patience and compassion, and if you have a true love for The Maker and The Almighty that reflects in your treatment of others, you will find Allah (s.w.t.) to be your Saviour, Salvation, and Guardian in this life and the next.

3rd Lesson

Allah (s.w.t.) seeks for us to re-establish the ties of kinship. This can be very difficult. Sometimes, our anger, pride, and arrogance get in the way, causing greater corruption than what we may have ever experienced. Allah (s.w.t.) warns us of this in Surah Yusuf, so we should take that counsel and observe similar behaviour in that regard.

Love & Sacrifice

Ayyub (a.s.)

The story of Ayyub (a.s.) is usually told from the perspective of patience, but in fact, it is also about the devoted love between him and his wife. Ayyub (a.s.) was a prophet of Allah, and some say that he resided among the Romans of the area. For fifty years, he lived a life of comfort and luxury, raising seven sons and seven daughters and enjoying many forms of wealth such as real estate, livestock, gold, and jewellery. Everyone in his community acknowledged him as their prophet; they had accepted the message because they associated his wealth, status, children, success, health, and good looks with the truth—until Allah (s.w.t.) began testing him and his people.

Allah (s.w.t.) sent the first test in the form of an earthquake that shook their land. His home collapsed, instantly killing all his children. But Ayyub (a.s.) was patient. Not long after, however, thieves entered his ranch and his home, stealing his livestock, torching his orchards, and murdering his servants. In just one night, Ayyub (a.s.) went from rich to bankrupt. Subsequently, his health began to deteriorate to the point that he grew so weak he could no longer stand. He could not pray as he normally did—he had to pray while laying down. His wife had to feed him, bathe him, and comb his hair for him.

In those trying times, everyone he knew departed, except his wife—she alone remained. All of a sudden, everyone who had believed in him now disbelieved in him as a prophet of Allah. *If this is happening to a prophet of Allah, that must mean the man is cursed*, they declared. *He must have committed a sin we are not aware of that has caused Allah to inflict him with this. Leave this man and do not believe a word from him.* They associated a life of luxury with the completion of faith.

Ibn Al-Qayyim explained that Allah (s.w.t.) giving us luxuries and happiness is a more difficult test—for us to pass to be safe in the *akhirah*—than Allah (s.w.t.) taking away things that we do not want to depart from. The more Allah (s.w.t.) gives us, the more accountable we are. Consider this: between those of us who are reading this and the struggling refugees camped on the borders of Syria, Jordan, or Turkey, who are more accountable?

Ayyub (a.s.) had everything stripped from him, and those who could not see with their hearts assumed that he was cursed by Allah (s.w.t.). His wife was the only one who remained with him through wealth and poverty, sickness and health, happiness and sorrow. She now had to work as a servant—going to people's houses to clean, cook, and wash for them—to help her husband.

After seven years of living in such difficult conditions, she asked her husband, Ayyub (a.s.), *Why don't you ask Allah to relieve you of this? You are a prophet of Allah, and you are a good man. If you simply say, "Ya Rabb," Allah will respond with a cure and will help you.*

So he asked her, *How many years of ease did we have?*

She replied, *Fifty*.

He asked again, *How long has this been?*

She said, *Seven*. In another narration, she said, *Seventeen*.

Ayyub (a.s.) said, *I am shy before my Lord. I am ashamed to ask Him for help and to be so impatient that I cannot at least repay that fifty years of happiness we had with some years of difficulty. I cannot ask Allah.*

She went quiet, suffering in silence with him. At that moment, Ayyub (a.s.) had not thought about her condition. There was a determination that led him to believe he could withstand more pain. All commentators of the *tafsir* say that the verses that what was taught to Ayyub (a.s.) prove he could have asked for Allah's mercy the moment difficulty struck, and yet he remained patient.

Eventually, the situation became worse. Nobody would hire his wife. *We do not want you to come*, they would say. *We are afraid that you will carry the curse into our house.*

She responded, *I have no food*, but from place to place, everyone shut their doors on her.

For days, they had nothing to eat. Finally, she went to Ayyub (a.s.) and requested that he ask Allah (s.w.t.) since no one was giving her any opportunity to work. However, Ayyub (a.s.) still refused.

The next day, she went out again to find someone who would give them something to eat. She came to a house, and a woman opened the door. Upon hearing her appeal, she said that she would give her food if she shaved her beautiful hair. The woman had a condition that caused her to lose her hair, and she wanted to make a wig out of it. Because of her love for her husband, Ayyub's wife made a sacrifice; she cut off all of her hair and gave it to the woman, and then she carried the food home.

Upon seeing the food in her hands, Ayyub (a.s.) asked, *What did you have to do for this?*

She refused to answer. He became angry, so she simply pulled her veil back to show him that she had cut her hair, and she walked away to go prepare the food. At that moment, Ayyub (a.s.) made a *du'a* (supplication), which Allah (s.w.t.) has recorded for us in the Qur'an:

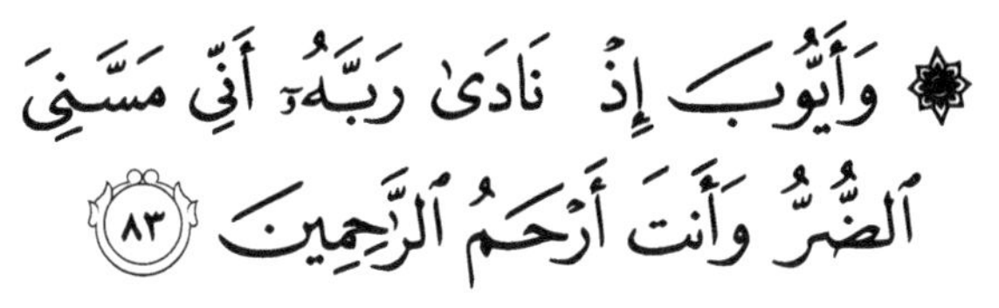

And [mention] Ayyub, when he called to his Lord, "Indeed, adversity has touched

me, and you are the Most Merciful of the merciful."
(Surah Al-Anbiya', 21:83)

Ayyub (a.s.) was moved by what he saw. He did not pity himself; he pitied her. His love for her was a reflection of her love for him. She had sacrificed something so valuable—her beauty—for him. Despite his own suffering, it was her suffering that he could not bear, since Allah (s.w.t.) had given him the power to change the situation. He understood; she had taught him a lesson of true love and sacrifice.

Immediately, Allah (s.w.t.) responded. Allah (s.w.t.) commanded him to touch the ground with his foot, and He said, *This is cleansing water so drink from it. It will cleanse you from within. Wash with it as it will change you.*

His wife had gone out, having left the sickly man in bed. When she came back in, a man was standing there. She could not recognise Ayyub (a.s.) because he looked much more like his younger self.

Who are you? she asked.

Just drink, he simply replied, and he gave her some water to drink and wash with.

Thereafter, Allah (s.w.t.) returned to Ayyub (a.s.) his family and everything he had lost, and He doubled them.

Allahu akbar! Seven sons became fourteen sons. Seven daughters became fourteen daughters. Estates increased into many more. The one city that previously believed in his prophethood grew into multiple cities of believers.

Abu Hurayrah (r.a.) narrated that the Prophet (s.a.w.) said,

بَيْنَمَا أَيُّوبُ عَلَيْهِ الصَّلَاةُ وَالسَّلَامُ يَغْتَسِلُ عُرْيَانًا خَرَّ عَلَيْهِ جَرَادٌ مِنْ ذَهَبٍ فَجَعَلَ يَحْثِي فِي ثَوْبِهِ قَالَ فَنَادَاهُ رَبُّهُ عَزَّ وَجَلَّ يَا أَيُّوبُ أَلَمْ أَكُنْ أَغْنَيْتُكَ قَالَ بَلَى يَا رَبِّ وَلَكِنْ لَا غِنَى بِي عَنْ بَرَكَاتِكَ

While Ayyub (a.s.) was bathing naked, locusts of gold landed on him, and he started to collect them in his garment. Then his Lord called him [saying], "O Ayyub, did I not make you rich?" He said, "Yes, O Lord, but I cannot do without Your blessing."
(*Sunan An-Nasa'i*)

With everything that Ayyub (a.s.) was given, he still did not want to let any portion of Allah's mercy depart from him, having learned this great lesson about appreciating His blessings.

The life of Ayyub (a.s.) holds many powerful messages of love, sacrifice, patience, fidelity, and the importance of a husband and wife walking through their difficulties.

The Lessons

1st Lesson

It is important for a husband and wife to connect and bear burdens as a team. Sometimes, we may think that our spouse is not doing enough, but it is easy to forget what they are actually doing for the family. We see each other as being insignificant when in fact we complement one another. We need to understand this lesson that Allah (s.w.t.) is giving us, especially in times of stress and hardship.

The story of Ayyub (a.s.) is a real-life experience. It changed his whole life, seeing his wife pulled back her veil to reveal her sacrifice. He could not wait for fifty years, not because he could not be patient until Allah's mercy descend upon him, but because of his compassion for his wife when seeing her in discomfort. To him, at that moment, her discomfort was of greater significance than the way he thought would be pleasing to Allah (s.w.t.).

2nd Lesson

If we observe patience and hold on to each other, although water may not gush forth from the earth to grant us longevity and restore our health, and pieces of gold may not rain down on us, perhaps we will be honoured by our children in our old age.

Perhaps by seeing us loving our spouse immensely and caring for each other, we will not worry if our children will go through marital conflicts because we modelled an example well. Nor will we worry about their children disrespecting the elders, because of the patience and endurance they saw in their parents and grandparents.

3rd Lesson

When the commentators of the Qur'an discussed which of the two spouses had shown greater patience, it was mentioned that although Ayyub (a.s.) was immensely patient as a prophet of Allah, one of the most important reflections of patience can be found in his wife. She fulfiled the role of someone deserving of a prophet of Allah, and Allah (s.w.t.) gave Ayyub (a.s.) someone who was a good fit for him, who would carry him through, support him, and assist him.

It is easy to forget that we are reflections of each other. Abu Hurayrah (r.a.) reported that the Prophet (s.a.w.) said,

الْمُؤْمِنُ مَرْآةُ أَخِيهِ، وَالْمُؤْمِنُ أَخُو الْمُؤْمِنِ، يَكُفُّ عَلَيْهِ ضَيْعَتَهُ، وَيَحُوطُهُ مِنْ وَرَائِهِ

A believer is the mirror of his brother. A believer is the brother of another believer. He protects him against loss and defends him behind his back.
(*Al-Adab Al-Mufrad*)

Just one word can change our spouse into our prosecutor. There is a switch that can turn the feelings of compassion, love, and care into frustration, anger, and disagreement. It is always that word, that comment, that attitude, that silent treatment—once we identify it, learn from it.

Hand in hand, Ayyub (a.s.) and his wife endured their hardship together, and this is the lesson that we can implement in our marriage.

4th Lesson

There is always going to be difficulties. If two people go into marriage thinking that married life would be an endless honeymoon, the moment there is a bump in the road, they give up on each other very quickly. They forget about perseverance and bearing patience together. These values are built into the story of Ayyub (a.s.).

Allah (s.w.t.) presents a very dramatic moment to us: when the wife of Ayyub (a.s.) asked him to make *du'a* to Allah (s.w.t.), he lost his patience. He said that if she continued to ask him, he would lash her one hundred times. Allah (s.w.t.) took this as an oath. When their lives and health were restored and filled with even more abundance, Allah (s.w.t.) commanded Ayyub (a.s.) to pick one hundred blades of grass and hit his wife with it once—because he had made that vow. It is almost as if Allah (s.w.t.) was disciplining Ayyub (a.s.).

Love & Tests

Dawud (a.s.)

When Dawud (a.s.) is first introduced to us, he was a young man, fifteen or sixteen years of age. Dawud (a.s.) had fair skin and blue eyes, and he spoke with a beautiful voice. He was diminutive but powerful, and he was one of the 4,000 men who crossed the Jordan river to battle against the greatest tyrants of Al-Almalikah. They were giants of the north, powerfully built, and their king was named Jalut (Goliath).

None of the soldiers from the army of Talut wished to face Jalut, except Dawud (a.s.). He put his hand up once, and twice, but they refused to let him fight. He offered himself the third time, and finally, they relented. He did not carry a sword or shield, but instead, he took with him a pebble. By the power of Allah (s.w.t.), he struck Jalut down, injuring him in the eye, causing his death. When the rest of the army saw the power of a single man from the army of Talut, they scattered away in retreat.

Dawud (a.s.) was married to the daughter of the king, and eventually, he inherited the throne. He became a prophet, a messenger, and a king for Bani Isra'il. He was an extraordinary leader; he never ate from anything except that he had worked for it. He did not take any tributes from his subjects; he went out and worked the land, made shields and armours from metal to sell, so that whatever accommodation and provision he had came from his own blood, sweat, and tears.

When he recited the scripture revealed to him, the Zabur (the Psalms), Allah (s.w.t.) would command the mountains to join him, reciting in unison. The birds would pause mid-flight to listen, and their wings would carry it everywhere. He was blessed with being able to recite the Zabur so well that the Prophet (s.a.w.) said,

خُفِّفَ عَلَى دَاوُدَ عَلَيْهِ السَّلاَمُ الْقُرْآنُ، فَكَانَ يَأْمُرُ بِدَوَابِّهِ فَتُسْرَجُ، فَيَقْرَأُ الْقُرْآنَ قَبْلَ أَنْ تُسْرَجَ دَوَابُّهُ، وَلاَ يَأْكُلُ إِلاَّ مِنْ عَمَلِ يَدِهِ

The reciting of the Zabur was made easy for Dawud (a.s.). He used to order that his riding animals be saddled and would finish reciting the Zabur before they were saddled. And he would never eat except from the earnings of his manual work.
(Sahih Al-Bukhari)

Dawud (a.s.) was not just an exceptional leader and a proficient reciter, he was also an excellent example of religious devotion. The Prophet (s.a.w.) commented about his fasting, saying,

أَفْضَلُ الصِّيَامِ صِيَامُ دَاوُدَ عَلَيْهِ السَّلَامُ كَانَ يَصُومُ يَوْمًا وَيُفْطِرُ يَوْمًا

The best of fasting is the fast of Dawud (a.s.). He used to fast for one day and break his fast for one day. (*Sunan an-Nasa'i*)

There is an account mentioned in Surah Al-Qasas about the test of Dawud (a.s.). It has a version that can be found in a book of Bani Isra'il; however, the most acceptable sources are the books of *tafsir*, such as *Tafsir Al-Qurtubi*, *Tafsir at-Tabari*, and others. There are, of course, some narrations that are false, and the account to follow uses the most correct narrations.

Every prophet of Allah was given a *du'a* that was answered for them. Dawud's *du'a* was, *O Allah, tell me the day when you will test me. I want to know which day you will test me so I can be ready, O Allah.* This was an audacious thought. So Allah (s.w.t.) tested Dawud (a.s.) with the test of the tests, and He told him what day it will be.

On the day Allah (s.w.t.) had set in His *qadr* (decree or destiny) that Dawud (a.s.) was fated to be tested severely, Dawud (a.s.) locked himself in his inner prayer chamber. There was only a small window at the top of the castle, which could not be accessed without climbing up the castle gate. He was prepared. He asked everyone not to disturb him, saying that he already had food and water with him. He wanted to minimise anything that could potentially test him. From the beginning of the day, Dawud (a.s.) did nothing but recite the Zabur, complete his prayer, and return to his recitation.

Then, a bird landed on the edge of his book, and he lifted his eyes to look at the bird as it flew out the window. From the window, he noticed a woman of beauty walking by. He said, *Masha'Allah*, and asked about her. They said that she was betrothed to be married to his general, who was defending their land at the bordering town, and that both of them would marry upon his return. Dawud (a.s.) thought to himself that if Allah (s.w.t.) gave that man *shahadah* (martyrdom), then he would certainly marry her.

Suddenly, two angels in the form of men climbed the wall, ascended through the window, and jumped in front of him. He was scared—the man who had slain Jalut was frightened.

The two of us are friends, they told Dawud (a.s.). *This man is like a brother to me. He has been blessed with ninety-nine sheep, and I have only one sheep. I have very little in comparison to him, but this brother wishes to take my sheep and possess them for himself, leaving none for me. Not one blessing.*

Dawud (a.s.) did not even listen to the other side of the story before giving his verdict. He said, *This man has wronged you by requesting your sheep when Allah has already given him so much.*

Immediately, Dawud (a.s.) understood what his test was. Out of respect, the Arabs would talk about a group of women as a flock of sheep, even in pre-Islamic poetry. *I am the man with the ninety-nine sheep. My general had little but that one sheep, and I still thought of taking it.* He turned to Allah (s.w.t.) in repentance, and Allah (s.w.t.) ends the story, saying,

يَٰدَاوُۥدُ إِنَّا جَعَلْنَٰكَ خَلِيفَةً فِى ٱلْأَرْضِ فَٱحْكُم بَيْنَ ٱلنَّاسِ بِٱلْحَقِّ وَلَا تَتَّبِعِ ٱلْهَوَىٰ فَيُضِلَّكَ عَن سَبِيلِ ٱللَّهِ ۚ إِنَّ ٱلَّذِينَ يَضِلُّونَ عَن سَبِيلِ ٱللَّهِ لَهُمْ عَذَابٌ شَدِيدٌۢ بِمَا نَسُوا۟ يَوْمَ ٱلْحِسَابِ ٢٦

O Dawud, I have sent you as a representative of truth and justice on this earth. So give verdicts in accordance with what is just; do not let your desire overcome

you because it will veer you off the truest path of Allah.
(Surah Sad, 38:26)

This is an extremely powerful image that Allah (s.w.t.) describes for us in this story in the Qur'an.

The Lessons

1st Lesson

It does not matter how pious you are or how high your *iman* (faith) is, each and every one of us is going to be tested by Allah (s.w.t.). Even Dawud (a.s.) asked when his test was coming, what it would be, and whether he would be successful or not. The Prophet (s.a.w.) concerned himself with spiritual nearness to Allah (s.w.t.). The prophets and messengers of Allah never took it for granted. They never said, *I am a messenger of Allah, and Jibril delivers a scripture to me. I know right from wrong, and Allah will help me.* Instead, Dawud (a.s.) recognised that this was his test.

We must understand that if a prophet of Allah like Dawud (a.s.) could be tested with such severity, our hearts will be tested too.

أَحَسِبَ ٱلنَّاسُ أَن يُتۡرَكُوٓاْ أَن يَقُولُوٓاْ ءَامَنَّا
وَهُمۡ لَا يُفۡتَنُونَ ﴿٢﴾ وَلَقَدۡ فَتَنَّا ٱلَّذِينَ مِن
قَبۡلِهِمۡۖ فَلَيَعۡلَمَنَّ ٱللَّهُ ٱلَّذِينَ صَدَقُواْ وَلَيَعۡلَمَنَّ
ٱلۡكَٰذِبِينَ ﴿٣﴾

Do the people think that they will be left to say, "We believe" and they will not be tried? But We have certainly tried those before them, and Allah will surely make evident those who are truthful, and He will surely make evident the liars.
(Surah Al-Ankabut, 29:2–3)

Through the tests of this life, Allah (s.w.t.) distinguishes the true believers from those who only claim to have faith but are deceitful.

2nd Lesson

Even great prophets take precautions to protect themselves from *fitnah* (trial). It may or may not work in our lives. There may be a temptation at our workplace, for example, in the form of a co-worker, money, fame, or peer pressure. We can see it, we can feel it—it is there. It is in our hearts. The Prophet (s.a.w.) reminded us,

تُعْرَضُ الْفِتَنُ عَلَى الْقُلُوبِ كَالْحَصِيرِ عُودًا عُودًا فَأَيُّ قَلْبٍ أُشْرِبَهَا نُكِتَ فِيهِ نُكْتَةٌ سَوْدَاءُ وَأَيُّ قَلْبٍ أَنْكَرَهَا نُكِتَ فِيهِ نُكْتَةٌ بَيْضَاءُ

Temptations will be presented to men's hearts as a reed mat is woven stick by stick, and any heart which is impregnated by them will have a black mark put into it, but any heart which rejects them will have a white mark put in it.
(*Sahih Muslim*)

It becomes our duty to prevent harm before it arrives. Sometimes, one can make the mistake of violating the rules of Islam and the norms of their culture that they have abided by their entire life—just for the sake of another person. The moment that happens, clearly something is wrong. They will know for themselves, and no one will need to tell them. So we must take preventive measures, like in the example of Dawud (a.s.), who locked himself in his prayer chamber when he knew a trial was going to happen.

3rd Lesson

We must always wish good for others. One of the things that injure our happiness is *hasad* (envy). It is when we are never satisfied with what we have that we end up with *hasad*.

4th Lesson

Allah (s.w.t.) will test us to the point of us coming to fault or success. Allah (s.w.t.) says in the Qur'an,

أَمْ حَسِبْتُمْ أَن تَدْخُلُوا۟ ٱلْجَنَّةَ وَلَمَّا
يَأْتِكُم مَّثَلُ ٱلَّذِينَ خَلَوْا۟ مِن قَبْلِكُم ۖ مَّسَّتْهُمُ

ٱلْبَأْسَآءُ وَٱلضَّرَّآءُ وَزُلْزِلُوا۟ حَتَّىٰ يَقُولَ ٱلرَّسُولُ
وَٱلَّذِينَ ءَامَنُوا۟ مَعَهُۥ مَتَىٰ نَصْرُ ٱللَّهِ ۗ أَلَآ إِنَّ
نَصْرَ ٱللَّهِ قَرِيبٌ ﴿٢١٤﴾

Or do you think that you will enter Paradise while such [trial] has not yet come to you as came to those who passed on before you? They were touched by poverty and hardship and were shaken until [even their] messenger and those who believed with him said,"When is the help of Allah?" Unquestionably, the help of Allah is near.
(Surah Al-Baqarah, 2:214)

The people of the past were tested with such severity that they came to a point where they started thinking, *When will Allah help us?* Allah (s.w.t.) will test us just like he tested the prophets and the nations before us.

But the most difficult of them is the test of faith. The Prophet (s.a.w.) would often make the following *du'a*:

وَلاَ تَجْعَلْ مُصِيبَتَنَا فِي دِينِنَا

And do not make our affliction in our...
...religion

(*Jami' At-Tirmidhi*)

We should always seek protection from being tested and having to struggle in our faithfulness to Allah (s.w.t.).

The Love of a Kingdom
Sulayman (a.s.)

It was mentioned in some books of *tafsir* that the woman Dawud (a.s.) saw from the window was married to him after the general she was betrothed to was martyred. Then came Sulayman (a.s.).

Sulayman (a.s.) was an environmentalist; when you hear his name mentioned in the Qur'an, in many cases, the narratives involve an animal. Everything around us—the creatures on the land and the birds in the skies—belongs to a nation of their own, not unlike we human beings. For each ant that we see around us, there are probably thousands more in colonies that we do not see. They communicate with sound, chemical signatures, and chemical trails. They have a social order: some of them are guardians, some of them are soldiers, some of them are workers, and some of them are diggers.

Imam Ibn Al-Qayyim has a chapter about the words of an ant in which he wrote nine blessings or functions of that one verse in Surah An-Naml. In verse 18 of the *surah*, Allah (s.w.t.) mentions, "...*An ant said*..." The use of the word "said" indicates that the ant spoke in a way that was meaningful to those who can hear it. Sulayman (a.s.) could hear and understand when the ant addressed the others, *Hurry to your place of abode and seek protection! Sulayman and his troops may trample you underneath their feet.*

Sulayman (a.s.) was given a kingdom like no one else had ever or would ever be given, except our Prophet,

Muhammad (s.a.w.). The evidence for this is recorded in *Sahih Al-Bukhari* and *Sahih Muslim*. One day, when the Prophet (s.a.w.) was in his *salah*, he made some movements as if he was holding something that was fighting him. Then, the Prophet (a.s.) released his hands and grew calm. The Prophet (s.a.w.) said, *Ifrit from the jinn came, seeking to distract me from my salah. So I held him and choked him. I thought of tying him to one of the pillars of the mosque so that all of you might see him, but I remembered the request of my brother, Sulayman, for no one to have such power other than him. Although it has been given it to me, I did not use it. So I released him for him to never return.*

Sulayman (a.s.) had control over the wind, the birds, the trees, and even the *jinns*—they would build, dive, and do all sorts of work under his command. One of the things that Sulayman (a.s.) enjoyed the most was the majestic stallions, as revealed in Surah Sad. Sulayman (a.s.) would speak to them and send them out to gallop around, and they would go from one end of the field to the other.

Some of the commentators of the Qur'an mention that one day, Sulayman (a.s.) was watching the stallions. It was after the time of '*asr* came. The two prayers that Bani Isra'il were ordered to perform were at the time of *fajr* and the time between '*asr* and *maghrib*—the two extremes of the day. As the sun was descending, Sulayman (a.s.) continued to be absorbed in the enjoyment of the *rizq* of Allah before him—until the sun had almost completely set and it was close to the time of *maghrib*. He nearly missed his prayer. Sulayman (a.s.) became so upset with himself that he said, *Take these horses away. I never want to see them again!* Some narrations say that the horses were slaughtered as a sacrifice to Allah (s.w.t.). He realised that he had fallen into the error of loving the goodness that Allah (s.w.t.) had blessed him with more than remembering to thank Him for the blessings.

The Lesson

Think about what we value in life. Perhaps there are certain things we love and esteem to a degree that should only be reserved to Allah (s.w.t.). We adore and treasure them so much that if they were taken away from us, our life would be destroyed.

Do not let our heart become too attached to anything other than Allah. However, that does not mean we should abandon all of the worldly pleasures and live in a dreary state of misunderstood contentment. Allah (s.w.t.) told us in the Qur'an,

وَلَا تَنسَ نَصِيبَكَ مِنَ ٱلدُّنْيَا ۖ

But seek, through that which Allah has given you, the home of the Hereafter; and [yet], do not forget your share of the world...
(Surah Al-Qasas, 28:77)

Where is the balance?

In an authentic *hadith* recorded in *Sahih Muslim*, the Prophet (s.a.w.) said that none shall enter *Jannah* if there is even a mustard seed of arrogance in their heart.

But what about those who like to wear fine clothing and footwear? A man asked.

The Prophet (s.a.w.) said, *Allah is The Source of beauty and finery in life, and He loves to see the effect of the blessings He has given you. This arrogance that I warn you of is that you reject truth on account of the one who carried it and that you look down upon the one who does not have what you have.*

Take a lesson from the example of Sulayman (a.s.). The kingdom that he asked for in his *du'a* to Allah (s.w.t.), *Give me a kingdom that no one can have the like of it after me*, became the thing that he asked Allah (s.w.t.) to protect him from as he said, *O Allah, this has distracted me from Your worship.*

Think. What distracts you from Allah (s.w.t.)? What keeps your heart away from Allah (s.w.t.)? The *dunya* is something you should enjoy living in, but do not ever seek to attain it at the expense of the *akhirah*.

Love & Honesty
Musa (a.s.)

The one drawn from the water—we all know the story of Musa (a.s.). But in this chapter, we will focus on the fascinating way in which he got married.

One day, Musa (a.s.) found two men in a heated quarrel. He intervened to save the one whom he thought was the victim in the situation, when in fact, the man was the perpetrator. Musa (a.s.) struck the other man, but the blow was too hard that he died as a result. Musa (a.s.) accidentally killed him. Musa (a.s.) said to himself, *This is evil.*

Despite Musa's good intentions, the man whom he tried to save began to use it against him. Another man soon came rushing to Musa (a.s.) with a bleak warning. *The people are conspiring against you, O Musa! Escape now while you still can, and I give you good advice.*

Musa (a.s.) escaped the city in fear, looking over his shoulder in worry. He then arrived in Madyan, a place we now refer to as northern Saudi Arabia. There is a mosque called Masjid Al-Khayf near Mina, and it is mentioned in a *hadith* that eighty prophets of Allah had prayed there, and one of them was Musa (a.s.). He made ten pilgrimages with those he lived with over there. When he discussed the marriage, they had a request. *Will you serve and stay with us for eight pilgrimage cycles? If you do ten, it will be kind of you.* We are not told what Musa (a.s.) said in response, but because it was him, we know that it was ten.

Musa (a.s.) came out of the desert with nothing. He was a refugee, homeless, and wanted for murder by the Egyptian army. As he entered into the clearing, he saw two young ladies being pushed away from their family well and their flock intentionally scattered into the desert. The sun was rising to its highest point, and because people of this lifestyle travelled nomadically from one well to the next, all those goats and sheep were going to die if they did not get water. Upon seeing the men causing difficulty to these women, he went to them, feeling concerned.

What is the problem? He asked.

We cannot get in the middle of these people, they said. *They keep scattering our sheep. They are abusing their place. It is not even their right to have this water before us.*

Immediately, Musa (a.s.) knew what to do, and the women witnessed the difference between a male (*dhakr*) person and a man (*rajul*).

Whenever Allah (s.w.t.) uses the word "*rajul*" in the Qur'an, it comes with qualifications. True men are established, standing on their own two feet in maintaining and caring for their women. Allah (s.w.t.) has put authority on one to be commanded so that they will be questioned in the service of the other. Allah (s.w.t.) will not hold a woman responsible for making an income to feed herself and her family, but He will hold a man responsible for not taking care of his family's financial situation. These are her rights to be taken care of, and it is his duty from Allah (s.w.t.) Himself to be truthful in the covenant they made to Him. In addition, true men are not distracted by their trade or their position from the remembrance of Allah.

When the two young women witnessed this act of chivalry from Musa (a.s.), they said to one another, *Masha'Allah.* When they went back home, they told their father, *Dear father, we found a good man. Can you hire him to work for us?*

The Prophet (s.a.w.) described Musa (a.s.) as a tall, powerfully built man, with dark skin and hair that looked like the wool on sheep. That was the man Allah (s.w.t.) chose to speak to without an angel in between.

One of the women went to see Musa (a.s.), saying, *Our father invites you so he can repay you for the kindness you showed us.*

Musa (a.s.) sent her back, not wanting to walk there alone with her. This was a test from her family that he had passed, making her father eager to meet Musa (a.s.) and wonder who the man was. Once Musa (a.s.) arrived, and the father had many questions for him. He began asking Musa (a.s.) with the same question that Musa (a.s.) asked his daughters, *What is the problem?*

This is where Surah Al-Qasas gets its name from: the stories. Musa (a.s.) went on to tell him the whole story—

everything. This is the nature of a truthful man, a prophet of Allah. That is in itself a great lesson.

The Lesson

The number one trait to look for when searching for a candidate for marriage is honesty, especially with the family. The reason that the man chose to marry his daughter to Musa (a.s.) was from seeing not just his honesty but also his open heart. He was a man who was willing to make known both his qualities and flaws, his failures and successes, truthfully—hoping that he would be judged by what he was doing instead of what he had done and that he would be accepted as he was now and would be in the future.

The Prophet (s.a.w.) said,

إِنَّ الصِّدْقَ يَهْدِي إِلَى الْبِرِّ، وَإِنَّ الْبِرَّ يَهْدِي إِلَى الْجَنَّةِ، وَإِنَّ الرَّجُلَ لَيَصْدُقُ حَتَّى يَكُونَ صِدِّيقًا، وَإِنَّ الْكَذِبَ يَهْدِي إِلَى الْفُجُورِ، وَإِنَّ

الْفُجُورَ يَهْدِي إِلَى النَّارِ، وَإِنَّ الرَّجُلَ
لَيَكْذِبُ، حَتَّى يُكْتَبَ عِنْدَ اللَّهِ كَذَّابًا

Truthfulness leads to righteousness, and righteousness leads to Paradise. And a man keeps on telling the truth until he becomes a truthful person. Falsehood leads to al-fajur (i.e., wickedness, evil-doing), and al-fajur (wickedness) leads to the (Hell) Fire, and a man may keep on telling lies till he is written before Allah, a liar.
(*Sahih Al-Bukhari*)

So, there are two stops: be truthful with Allah (s.w.t.), with yourself, and with the people, and you will become righteous; your righteousness will lead you into *Jannah*. On the other hand, dishonesty will lead you to *Jahannam* (Hellfire).

In a *hadith* recorded in *Sahih At-Tirmidhi*, after teaching about some of the laws of Islam, the Prophet (s.a.w.) said to Mu'adh (r.a.), *Shall I not tell you what is the foundation of all that?*

Mu'adh (r.a.) replied, *Of course, O Prophet of Allah.*

The Prophet (s.a.w.) took hold of his tongue and said, *Control this.*

Mu'adh (r.a.) said, *O Prophet of Allah, will we be held responsible for what we say with it?*

The Prophet (s.a.w.) said, *May your mother be bereft of you, O Mu'adh! Will the people be thrown into Hell on their faces or on their noses for anything other than the harvest of their tongues?*

Honesty is the pillar of every healthy relationship, whether it is in your workplace or with your loved ones—your children, your spouse, or your parents. We must always look for an opportunity to rise in truth and to make known the rights of people. Stand up with the words of truth and equity for Allah's sake, even if it is against yourself.

Love in the Long Distance
Ibrahim (a.s.)

As a young boy, Ibrahim (a.s.) used to follow his father to the quarry. His father would ask him to pick up a rock to make a god with.

Ibrahim (a.s.) would ask, *Father, this rock and that rock look the same. They are from the same area. What makes this rock more godly than that rock?*

Instead of getting an answer, young Ibrahim would be smacked and told not to ask anything.

To his mother, young Ibrahim would ask, *Mom, who do I have to listen to?*

She would say, *Me.*

Next, he would ask, *Who do you listen to?*

She would say, *Your dad.*

Next, he would ask, *Who does he listen to?*

She would say, *The king.*

Next, he would ask, *Who does the king listen to?*

Instead of getting an answer, young Ibrahim would be smacked and told not to think too much.

One day, Ibrahim (a.s.) asked his father, *Father, this thing you made—does it hear you? Remember the rock I carried? It could not move on its own. I had to carry it—it was very heavy. So now it is here. You beat it, you carved it, and you made this thing. Does this thing hear us? Does it see us? How does it help us? Does it even move or do anything?*

His father said, *Listen, boy. If you do not stop with these questions, I am going to stone you. This is what my father taught me. I am giving you the keys to the castle here. Son, listen up and pay attention. You are going to live a good life if you listen to me. When it does not rain, the king comes to me—he is only a king because I made him king—when he needs me to do a rain dance or make an offering to ask God for rain, he comes to me. Do not listen to your mother that I listen to the king; he listens to me. Bring this. We are going. There's a festival today.*

Ibrahim (a.s.) said, *Father, I am feeling sick.*

His father responded, *Actually, it's better that you don't come. You're only going to embarrass me in front of the people. You talk too much, and you ask too many silly questions.*

In truth, Ibrahim (a.s.) was not sick. He lied. In a *hadith* recorded in *Sahih Al-Bukhari*, Abi Sa'id Al-Khudri (r.a.) narrated the Prophet (s.a.w.) saying that on the Day of Judgement, when we come to Prophet Ibrahim (a.s.) and ask him to save us, he will say, *Go to someone else. I lied three times in my life. I am scared for myself. So go to someone else.*

He lied that he was sick because he had a plan. When everyone was at the festival, he went to the place of the idols. He knew they were powerless. With his strong right hand, he broke them all except one—the biggest one.

When the people return, they were all shocked. *Who did this?*

Some from among them said, *We know of this young boy named Ibrahim who had been talking about them.*

Look at how they gave his father reverence; they did not say, *It is the priest's son*, even though they knew exactly who Ibrahim (a.s.) was.

Ibrahim (a.s.) was called over, and they interrogated him. *Did you do this to our gods?*

No, no, no. Let me tell you what happened. It was the big one. I saw the big one running after the smaller ones, smashing them and destroying them. Ask them!

He gave them his story. At that moment, the people understood that they had been infected with *shirk* (making partners with Allah) all this while. Allah (s.w.t.) tells us in Surah Al-Anbiya' that they came back to their senses themselves. Inside their mind, they reconciled what they had just heard.

This boy is making a mockery of us. Obviously, they cannot speak—they cannot do anything. We know they do not do anything. It clicked in their mind.

Who was the one who stopped them from coming to the faith? It was Ibrahim's own father.

He said, *Burn him and help your gods!*

So they built the biggest fire ever and catapulted Ibrahim (a.s.) into the flame. But Allah (s.w.t.) saved him by commanding the fire to be cool and peaceful for Ibrahim (a.s.). In some of the narrations, everything that was binding him was burnt, but his body and clothing were not. He walked out of the flame untouched. He went back and comforted his mother, telling her that he was fine.

However, even after witnessing the miracle, the people were still reluctant to accept the truth. They exiled him from his homeland, and his own father renounced him. Anyone in his position would no longer be able to love and be hopeful for their father—someone who is supposed to love you and nurture you, protect you and support you—without any bitterness or resentment. But Ibrahim (a.s.), being the forbearing son he was, continued to make *du'a* for his father. *My Lord, forgive my father. Indeed, he is misguided.*

The *du'a* that we recite after our *salah* is the *du'a* of Ibrahim (a.s.) for the man who threw him into the fire, the same man who led the whole society away from Allah (s.w.t.). Regardless of what happened between them, Ibrahim (a.s.) continued to love his father from long distance. He continued to make *du'a* to Allah (s.w.t.), *O Allah, lead him to good. O Allah, forgive him for what he did to me. O Allah, forgive him for his shirk and for misleading his people.* For as long as he had a breath in his life, Ibrahim (a.s.) never gave up hope—until his father passed away.

The Lessons

1st *Lesson*

Sometimes, we give up on people too soon. The mind that is diseased with extremism will look at others judgingly, thinking they can never be worthy of any redemption or any hope with Allah (s.w.t.).

One of the famous scholars of the past, Imam Ibn Al-Jauzy (r.h.)—he was not only a scholar of *hadith* but also a poet and a warrior—used to teach some of his students on the bank of the Euphrates river in Iraq. One day, on the other side of the river was a group of young people, men and women, frolicking in drunkenness and sin. His students said to him, *Make du'a that Allah does something with these people.*

So he raised his hand and said, *O Allah, as you gave them joy in this life, give them greater joy in the akhirah.*

Imam Ibn Al-Jauzy (r.h.) did not condemn them, but rather, he asked Allah (s.w.t.) to bless them with repentance and faith so that they could have joy in the *akhirah*.

Sometimes, our hearts are so trapped in hatred that we cannot pray for someone who has wronged us—not even for a person close to us. Look at the example of Ibrahim (a.s.). *O Allah, forgive my father. He was misguided.* Ibrahim (a.s.) continued making this *du'a* until Allah (s.w.t.) told him that there was no hope for his father to come to the faith; only then, he stopped doing so.

2nd Lesson

In life, there is symmetry. The same ordeal that Ibrahim (a.s.) had to endure as a son, must be endured by his son.

His own father wanted to kill him. The father's heart is naturally inclined towards loving and protecting his offspring. To throw all those feelings away and pursue the killing of his own son—how misguided could he be? How blinded was he?

Allah (s.w.t.) showed Ibrahim (a.s.) how difficult that was for his father. This was why he continued to make *du'a* for his father despite everything—because Allah (s.w.t.) tested him with something very similar.

Ibrahim (a.s.) had a dream in which Allah (s.w.t.) ordered him to slaughter his son, Isma'il (a.s.). He went to him and said, *Come, we have to go.* As Ibrahim (a.s.) was obedient to his father, Allah (s.w.t.) blessed him with an obedient son, who was righteous as he was righteous. This is the symmetry of life.

If you care for your parents and make *du'a* for them, Allah (s.w.t.) will bless you with children who will care for you and make *du'a* for you. Perhaps you might not be worthy or your parents might not be worthy, perhaps they were not the best father or the best mother, or perhaps there were troubles and difficulties in the family—do not let any of that stop you from loving them, being kind to them, and doing your best for them. Because, remember, as you do will be done to you.

3rd Lesson

Allah (s.w.t.) tests us with the same test that we have caused others. When you see yourself acting in a way that causes stress and difficulties in someone else's life—when you become a source of *fitnah*—know without a doubt that the same trial will manifest itself to you in a different circumstance and at a different time in your life.

Imam Ibn Al-Qayyim (r.h.) cautioned us with a reminder, saying, *The one who looks at a person and mocks them for a sin, their punishment in the dunya is that they will fall into that sin.* May Allah (s.w.t.) protects us.

The Love of the Two Mothers
Musa (a.s.)

Many times, when Allah (s.w.t.) is going to test us in life, He provides precursors and warnings. We should make it a standard in our lives to be on the lookout for signs Allah (s.w.t.) gives us that *fitnah* is about to arrive. Allah (s.w.t.) reminds us in the Qur'an,

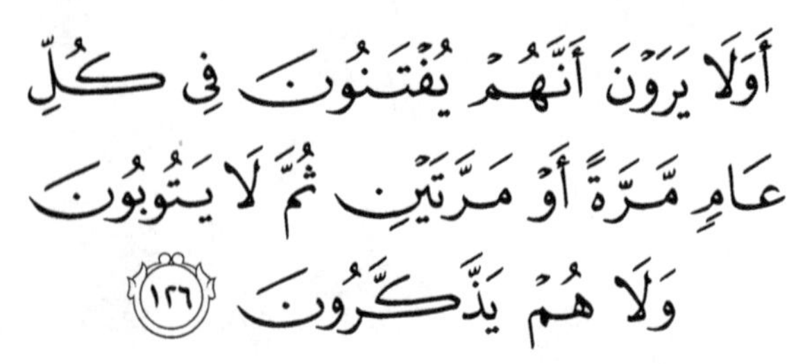

Do they not see that they are tried every year once or twice, but then they do not repent nor do they remember?
(Surah Tawbah, 9:126)

Fir'awn had seen a dream with a warning—even though he was a tyrant, Allah (s.w.t.) still warned him. The dream indicated that his *fitnah* was coming, and his power and time was nearly at its end. There would be a rising star from among Bani Isra'il who would destroy his kingdom and reclaim the power for Allah (s.w.t.). Thereafter, Fir'awn put out the order that every male child born into Bani Isra'il to be executed.

The biological mother of Musa (a.s.) was a righteous woman. She carried him at a time when the killing order was enforced, and she began to see dreams of soldiers coming to her home seeking to end the life of her blessed child.

Allah (s.w.t.) described the story perfectly and eloquently in the Qur'an in Surah Al-Qasas. The great scholars of *tafsir* said that there is no verse of the Qur'an that is more prolific in its Arabic grammar, poetry, and beauty than in Surah Al-Qasas. It is the verse that has silenced even the greatest poets.

Labid, a distinguished poet, the most illustrious of the Arabs at the time, heard this *ayah* as he walking by a young slave girl reciting Qur'an in the street. He sat on the ground and listened.

Where did you get this? he asked after she finished.

It is the book of Allah, she replied.

This man whose poetry was once hung on the very walls of the Ka'bah in pre-Islamic Arabia wholeheartedly submitted to Allah (s.w.t.) upon hearing this recitation.

Allah (s.w.t.) says in the *surah*,

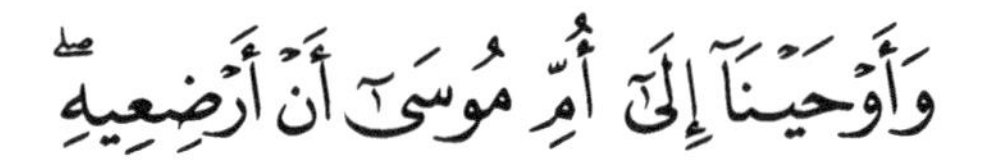

And We inspired to the mother of Musa...
(Surah Al-Qasas, 28:7)

Can you imagine how deeply righteous was this lady, that Allah (s.w.t.) would divinely intervene through her dreams?

And Allah (s.w.t.) continues,

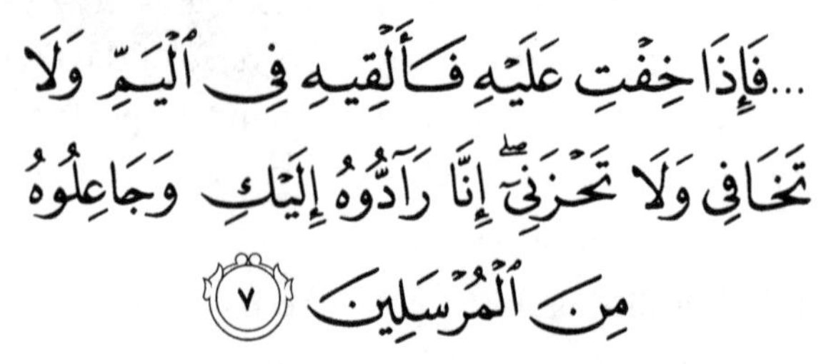

...Suckle him; but when you fear for him, cast him into the river and do not fear and do not grieve. Indeed, We will return him to you and will make him [one] of the messengers.
(Surah Al-Qasas, 28:7)

In that one verse, Allah (s.w.t.) makes two prohibitions, two glad tidings, and two predictions of the future. *Allahu akbar*, how profound!

After Musa (a.s.) was born, his mother prepared the basket and tested it. When the time came, she pushed it down the river, with him inside. When she sent the basket down the Nile, she believed as it was revealed in her dream that her son was going to be spared from Fir'awn. However, when she saw that the basket was carried by the current towards Fir'awn's castle—not away from it—she was distressed. Allah (s.w.t.) recounts the moment,

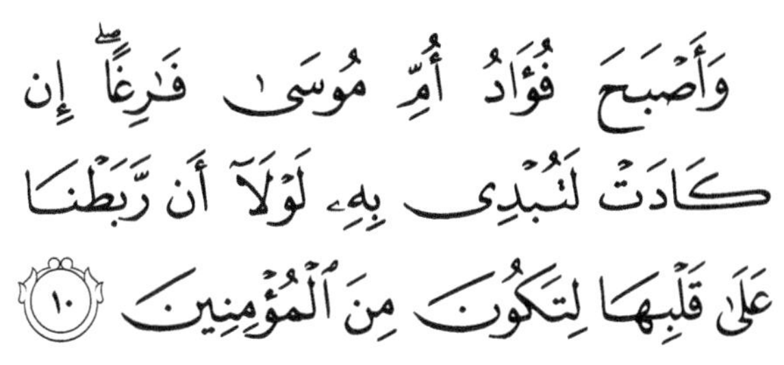

And the heart of Musa' mother became empty (of all else). She was about to disclose (the matter concerning) him had We not bound fast her heart that she would be of the believers.
(Surah Al-Qasas, 28:10)

According to some narration, the woman who picked up Musa (a.s.) from the river was his second mother, Asiya, the wife of Fir'awn. She grabbed the baby—who was clearly not from her people as he had darker complexion—and took him to her husband.

I am keeping him, she told Fir'awn.

Fir'awn was the very Pharaoh who had ordered the killing of all male newborns from his slaves, Bani Isra'il, and yet on his doorstep was a child from them. He refused, but she insisted.

She looked at Fir'awn, saying, *We are keeping him.*

Asiya did not have a child of her own, but she became the guardian of a great messenger of Allah. She looked at Fir'awn, the tyrant, squarely in the face and stood up to him with the simple words, *I am keeping him.* When he said, *No*, she said, *Yes*. This is the reality of life, and Allah (s.w.t.) teaches us this in the Qur'an.

Here, we should see the love of Allah for our mothers. The story of love that we are discussing in this chapter is not one of Musa (a.s.) himself. It is not about Allah (s.w.t.) protecting him. It is about Allah's love for the mother of Musa (a.s.).

Allah (s.w.t.) had already saved Musa. If he was to be kept with his new mother, who would take him under her care and he was to become a messenger of Allah, it would be sufficient. But Allah (s.w.t.) looked into the heart of his real mother and saw the emptiness and sorrow she held. Out of love for her—and to elevate our Muslim sisters, mothers, aunts, and so on—Allah (s.w.t.) says,

فَرَدَدْنَٰهُ إِلَىٰٓ أُمِّهِۦ كَىْ تَقَرَّ عَيْنُهَا وَلَا تَحْزَنَ وَلِتَعْلَمَ أَنَّ وَعْدَ ٱللَّهِ حَقٌّ وَلَٰكِنَّ أَكْثَرَهُمْ لَا يَعْلَمُونَ ١٣

So We restored him to his mother that she might be content and not grieve and that she would know that the promise of Allah is true.
(Surah Al-Qasas, 28:13)

Allahu akbar! Ponder upon this. How dare we use a single moment in our lives to bring sadness to the heart of our mother—our parent—when Allah (s.w.t.) divinely intervened to bring joy to the heart of the mother? And it was not for Musa (a.s.), but for her—because it is from Allah's love for her that she did not have any sadness, but instead experiences joy in her heart.

The Lessons

1st Lesson

Revelation carries a different meaning for different beings. For example, Allah (s.w.t.) gives revelation to animals, such as the bees. In Surah An-Nahl, Allah (s.w.t.) says,

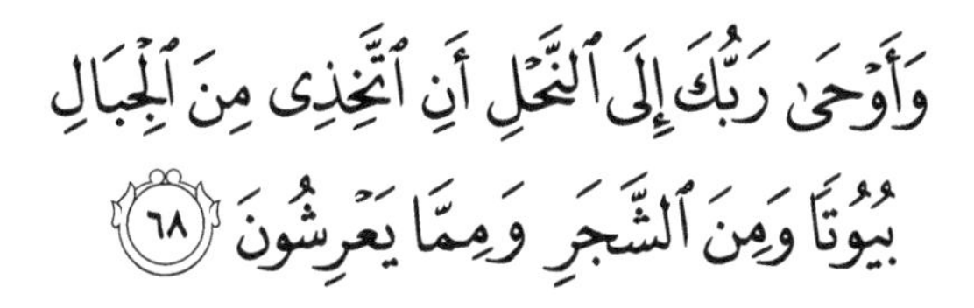

And your Lord inspired to the bee, "Take for yourself among the mountains, houses, and among the trees and (in) that which they construct."
(Surah An-Nahl, 16:68)

The *shaytan* can also give revelation; they descend upon the heart and inspire the words of deception. Therefore, much of what we see at times are not entirely the fault of human beings themselves, but they are from the inspiration of the *shaytan.*

And thirdly, Allah (s.w.t.) gives revelation through dreams. An example can be seen in this story of the mother of Musa (a.s.) who had dreams that revealed the future to her.

2nd Lesson

At times, we misunderstand the principles of our *deen (religion)*. What was once clear in the Qur'an to those in the past has become obscure to many of us. Something we hear often as members of the Muslim community is that Muslim women are not valued enough. However, in our *deen*, being gifted a daughter is a greater *rahmah* (mercy) than being gifted a son.

The *scholars* comment on the matter of sacrificing two sheep for the son and only one sheep for the daughter Allah (s.w.t.) has blessed a family with. Some people may say, *Look at these Muslims; for the female, they give less meat.* In reality, the concept is that to have a son is a *fitnah*—we must make a greater offering to ask Allah (s.w.t.) for greater *barakah* in order to pass this test that is greater than the test of having a daughter. In an authentic *hadith*, the Prophet (s.a.w.) said,

مَنِ ابْتُلِيَ مِنْ هَذِهِ الْبَنَاتِ بِشَيْءٍ
فَأَحْسَنَ إِلَيْهِنَّ كُنَّ لَهُ سِتْراً مِنَ النَّارِ
متفقٌ عَلَيهِ

He who is involved [in the responsibility] of [bringing up] daughters, and he is benevolent towards them, they would become protection for him against Hellfire. (*Sahih Al-Bukhari* & *Sahih Muslim*)

The daughters will be a barrier between their parents and *Jahannam*, if the parents raised them with sound ethics and manners, without preferring their brothers over them in treatment or in value.

When Imam Ahmad received news that someone's wife had given birth to a daughter, he would write them a congratulatory note saying, *Welcome, you are now amongst the level of the prophets of Allah in the children they were given. Prophet Muhammad (s.a.w.) was a father of daughters.*

Of the greatest blessings we have is that Muslim women are the ones to bring about the rectification of our *ummah* (society).

The mother of Maryam (a.s.) once made a *du'a*, *O Allah, I am carrying a child. I am going to commit this child to You.* She thought it would be a son, and she was hoping that he would become a leader for Bani Isra'il. When she gave birth to a female, she said, *O Allah, I gave birth to a daughter.* She underestimated the power and elevation of what she had been gifted by Allah (s.w.t.).

The boy she wanted could never be equal to this girl. If she had had a son, he could never have achieved what Maryam (a.s.) had achieved. Look at the words of the Qur'an: Maryam, the daughter of 'Imran. It is not Maryam, the mother of 'Isa. Her claim to status was not based on being the mother of a prophet; it was based on who she was. Khadijah (r.a.) was the wife of Muhammad (s.a.w.), but she was known as the daughter of Khuwaylid and a distinguished, devoted worshipper of Allah (s.w.t.), not just on the account of her marriage to the Prophet (s.a.w.).

The mother of Musa (a.s.) became the example of the love of Allah for our sisters, mothers, daughters, and wives.

3rd Lesson

The love of Allah follows the love of your parents. In the book *Al-Kaba'ir*, Imam Adh-Dhahabi mentioned that Musa (a.s.) asked Allah (s.w.t.) who his neighbour in Paradise will be. Allah (s.w.t.) informed him that his neighbour will be a butcher. Musa (a.s.) wanted to meet this man, so Allah (s.w.t.) instructed him to travel and he would find the man by a river, selling meat.

Musa (a.s.) watched from a distance to see what was so special about this man. After butchering the meat, the man would keep part of the meat and sell the rest.

Musa (a.s.) approached him in the late afternoon, saying, *I am a traveller, and I need a place to stay. May I accompany you?*

The man replied, *Yes, you may follow me, but I will be busy. Wait until I have finished preparing things. Then, I will give you more attention.*

When they reach the man's home, he entered and brought down a large basket from an elevated platform—in it was a frail, elderly woman. He carried the basket down to the river, bathed the old woman, washed her clothes, dressed her, combed her hair, and put perfume on her. The butcher then sat her by the fire as he cooked for her the best quality meat he had. As soon as the meat was ready, he began to cut the meat and chewed on pieces of it. Once it was soft enough, he placed the meat into the sickly old woman's mouth. With every bite, her lips would move in supplication. After she was content, he brought the basket and returned it to the platform, and she fell asleep.

Only then he turned to Musa (a.s.).

Welcome. Let me provide you with attention and what you deserve from me.

Before we begin, who is this? Musa (a.s.) inquired.

This is my mother, the man replied.

How long have you been serving her?

Ten years.

When you feed her, what does she whisper? asked Musa (a.s.). *I could not hear.*

She makes du'a for me.

Yes, but what du'a?

She says, O Allah, make my son with the prophets of Allah.

In a *hadith* reported by 'Abdullah Ibn 'Amr (r.a.), the Prophet (s.a.w.) said,

رِضَى الرَّبِّ فِي رِضَى الْوَالِدِ
وَسَخَطُ الرَّبِّ فِي سَخَطِ الْوَالِدِ

The pleasure of the Lord is in the pleasure of the parents, and the displeasure of the Lord is in the displeasure of the parents.
(*Sunan At-Tirmidhi*)

Imam An-Nawawi and others, when explaining the second part of this *hadith*, commented that it is regardless of whether the wrath of our parents is deserved or undeserved. Sometimes we are innocent, and we have not done anything sinful that upset them; however, the fact that Allah (s.w.t.) would move their hearts in anger towards us is a sign that there is an imbalance between you and Allah (s.w.t.). Therefore, we need to open our hearts.

4th Lesson

Allah (s.w.t.) had destined in the *qadr* of Asiya, the wife of Fir'awn, that she could not bear any children of her own. However, Allah had also destined for her to become the second mother of His prophet, Musa (a.s.). *SubhanAllah*!

This is a lesson for the sisters of today. Some sisters will carry their own children, whereas some will carry *barakah* for other people.

The teacher of our teachers, the great *qari'ah* (reciter of Qur'an), Umm Sa'ad of Alexandria, Egypt, is an exceptional example of this phenomena. No *imam* (leader) who recites the Qur'an with authority in our times—from Imam Abdul Basit Abdul Samad to Al-Menshawy, to Al-Mustafa Ismail, or any others—has ever been given the authority to recite unless their *sanad* (chain of narration) came from Umm Sa'ad. That is how distinguished her authority was on the recitation of the Qur'an.

In the final year of her life, she used to say, *Alhamdulillah, I am thankful to Allah who protected me from having my own children*—she was never blessed with having a child—*and that Allah gave me the freedom that I could work for the deen and teach Qur'an. Allahu akbar*!

The Love of a Father
Luqman Al-Hakim

Luqman (a.s.) was referred to as Al-Hakim, the wise. The greatest *hikmah* (wisdom) of Luqman (a.s.) is when he was asked what wisdom is. He said, *You have to be conscious of Allah. Whatever you do in life, you measure it by what Allah seeks and what you are willing and able to do, seeking Allah's pleasure.*

The clearest definition of the word *taqwa* (piety) is that we use our capacity and strength to obey God, through the light that He sent us: the book of Allah and the tradition of the Prophet (s.a.w.). We seek His reward by abandoning sin, with our greatest capacity and guided by the light, in hope that we will be saved from His punishment.

Luqman was not a king, a messenger, or a prophet—he was a slave. Yet, a chapter of the Qur'an was named after him. It was how he nurtured his heart with knowledge, certainty, and the love of Allah that elevated his status and gave him insight into the inner workings of life. He would see what the eyes could not see because he saw the world with his heart.

Allah (s.w.t.) tells us in the Qur'an,

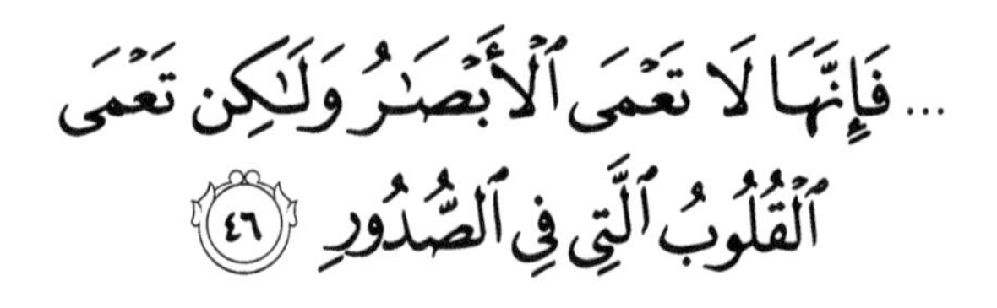

*...For indeed, it is not eyes that are blinded,
but blinded are the hearts which are within
the breasts.*
(Surah Al-Hajj, 22:46)

We can a find a slave, an illiterate, or a person with little sense or knowledge, but their hearts lead them like a compass away from the trials of life and back to Allah (s.w.t.). Luqman (a.s.) was one of these people.

We spoke about the relationship between a mother and her son in the previous chapter. Here, we move on to the bond between a father and his child.

Luqman (a.s.) said to his son, *My dear son, do not ever make anyone equal to Allah. Do not ever turn your attention to other than Allah.*

Sometimes, this concept of *shirk* can be misunderstood. Many Muslims see *shirk* as someone worshipping an idol, but *shirk* is that you put yourself or something else where only Allah (s.w.t.) should be, that you love someone in a way that only Allah (s.w.t.) should be loved, and that you seek from others what you should only seek from Allah (s.w.t.).

My dearest son, do not ever think of me as an authority in your life greater than Allah. Do not ever lie to me to save yourself from me and think that you have hidden it from Allah.

Sometimes, we reinforce the wrong things with our children seeking a proper practice of faith. A father may come home and say to his son, *Did you pray 'Asr?* They will say, *Yes*—even if it is a lie—out of fear of what the father will do or say. In between them and Allah (s.w.t.), however, it is not true. This just reinforces unhealthy and negative behaviour. Instead, he should say, *If you haven't prayed 'Asr, join me because I haven't prayed yet either.* This is a completely different way of presenting what one seeks from Allah (s.w.t.), without being someone who is to be feared.

My dearest son, from the very beginning, do not make me or yourself or anyone else in a place that only Allah should be, the central in your life, because the greatest injustice is to make anything in partner with Allah.

Then, we find a shift in the transmission. After Luqman (a.s.) advised his son to worship Allah (s.w.t.) alone and not make anyone a partner with Him, Allah (s.w.t.) Himself speaks.

I say to you, all mankind, to be good to your parents.

Therefore, it is as if Allah (s.w.t.) is saying that after the worship of Allah and eliminating *shirk* from your life, there should be no greater love, obedience, or relationship that you have in your life than to your parents. To clarify further, Allah (s.w.t.) says that even those parents who try to force you to commit *shirk* have equal rights for your love and care—He does not speak only of those parents who are easy to love or to follow.

If you have the misfortune of having parents who combat you and struggle against you so that you will commit shirk, to bring you away from Me, do not obey them in this; but be their sahabi in the dunya.

We must be to our parents the way Abu Bakr (r.a.) was to Muhammad (s.a.w.), even to those parents who make *jihad* (struggle) against our *iman*. Look at the words of Allah—He interjects between the advice of Luqman (a.s.) for us to understand what is next of importance.

Luqman (a.s.) went on to say, *My son, if whatever deed you perform, even if it was an atom's weight of good or bad, and you were to hide it in the heaven or the earth, under the rocks or wherever; Allah will bring it forward. Nothing is hidden from Him. It is not me you should be concerned about. It is not the thoughts of others about you that you should be worried about. It is not the others', but it is Allah's. It is to build that ihsan where although you do not see Allah, you know that He witnesses you at all times.*

My dearest son, be regular in your prayers.

Learn what is good and teach it to others. Learn what is wrong and prohibited upon us and protect yourself and others from it.

Look at the advice of a father who loved his son: worship Allah (s.w.t.) alone, be good to your parents, remember that Allah (s.w.t.) sees and knows everything you do, be regular in your prayers, enjoin what is good, and condemn what is evil. We would say, *subhanAllah*, what a beautiful child if they can achieve all that—surely they will have a blessed and easy life.

But Luqman (a.s.) was the one with wisdom. He spoke to his son as if saying that if you pray, do good and lead others to good, avoid evil and lead others away from evil, the consequence of that righteousness is one thing: be patient in what Allah (s.w.t.) will cause to befall you—hardship will follow you in life.

It sounds strange. A person may say, *I pray, I fast, I am generous, and in everything in my life, I seek the path of Allah and what is equitable. In everything I seek from Allah, I seek to do the best that I can. So why is my life full of difficulties and hurdles?*

That hardship is love from Allah (s.w.t.).

Love is not easy, and *barakah* is not about Allah (s.w.t.) giving us whatever we want, whenever we want. *Barakah* is that we struggle to achieve what is best even though we do not know if it is indeed the best. It is to live like Ibrahim (a.s.), who left his wife and their newborn son in a place void of vegetation and water—but that land is actually the land of *barakah* because, in that land, they would soon be able to establish the prayer and find what they want later on in life. So the best advice for a person in hardship is to be patient in light of this knowledge.

The Lessons

1st *Lesson*

A life lesson to take from this story of the love between a father and son is that love is not in the words, but it is in the actions. It is about the father taking his son by the hand and walking him to the mosque. It is about the father following the child's growth in their behaviour and their lives. It is the established practice of a loving, supportive demeanour—not just empty words.

Let's look at another example. The beauty of a *hadith* is not necessarily from the wording of the *hadith* itself; its beauty can also be found from the chain of narration. 'Abdullah ibn 'Umar (r.a.) was one of the greatest *muhaddith* (reporters of *hadith*) from the *sahabah*, and he lived for more than a decade with the Prophet (s.a.w.), narrating more than 3,000 *ahadith* from him, which makes him the fourth—if not the third—most prolific reporters narrating directly from the Prophet (s.a.w.).

And yet, in the first *hadith* recorded in *Sahih Muslim*, 'Abdullah ibn 'Umar (r.a.) did not narrate from the Prophet (s.a.w.) directly. He began the *hadith* by saying, *My father told me...* and not *The Messenger of Allah (s.a.w.) said.*

So why did someone like 'Abdullah ibn 'Umar (r.a.), who lived with and ate with the Prophet (s.a.w.), need to learn and share knowledge from anyone other than him (s.a.w.)? The answer is that the primary source of nurture and knowledge for a child must always be the parents.

As fathers, many of us are not fully present in observing our duties. We believe that it is the mother's responsibility to take charge of all the education of our children, be it math, science, or Qur'an. We put shared responsibilities on our wives and on others whom we assume will be enough to facilitate the need to raise them well. *My job is just to pay for it and to fulfil their basic needs. That is enough.*

The reality is that even someone living in the presence of the Messenger of Allah (s.a.w.) needed to be guided and commanded by his father.

2nd Lesson

What Luqman (a.s.) sought to teach his son is something we fail to instil in our children, that is, to be able to delay gratification. We must teach our children to wait for what is good and endure with resilience and tenacity in the moments of difficulty in life.

SubhanAllah, sometimes we think that we show love to our children by facilitating provision, but rather it is the opposite. Everything in our *deen* is about learning to wait. Look at the words of Allah in a *hadith qudsi* (saying of Allah through Prophet Muhammad [s.a.w.]),

وَلِلصَّائِمِ فَرْحَتَانِ: فَرْحَةٌ حِينَ يُفْطِرُ،
وَفَرْحَةٌ حِينَ يَلْقَى رَبَّهُ

He who fasts has two joys: a joy when he breaks his fast and a joy when he meets his Lord.
(*Sahih Al-Bukhari*)

We fast and we become hungry, yet we patiently wait for that moment where we will have happiness.

It is important to provide our children with the understanding that just because they can do what they want, it does not mean that they should or must do it. Nor does it mean that anything they want is an immediate need. There has to be a challenge in life, and there has to be a purpose that drives you towards your aspiration.

In the 1950s and the 1960s, researchers conducted a psychological test called the Marshmallow Test. They brought children from ages three to four into a room, sitting them at a desk. Cameras recorded the experiment without their knowledge. The children were kept from eating lunch, so they were hungry. Then, the researchers put a marshmallow in front of them, and they were given a simple instruction.

I am going to my office. This is yours, and you can have it now. But if you can wait until I return from my office, I will give you another one.

Some children had already grabbed and gobbled up the marshmallow impulsively before the adult had even left the room. There were others who were deceptive; they would lick it, bite it, and nibble on it. The final fifteen per cent, however, were able to delay gratification for a greater return; they would put the marshmallow at the far corner of their desk, covering it with a cup so they could not smell it, or turning their faces away so they would not see it. By the end of the experiment, they had done whatever they could to resist and hold on, and they were given another piece of marshmallow. One girl even asked, *If I wait for longer, will you give me another?*

What they found after following these children for the next forty years was that the fifteen per cent grew up to be people with higher education level and greater savings, allowing them to become leaders in their industry and live in prosperity. On the other hand, the impulsive or deceptive children grew up to be people who were less likely to have good savings, keep a job for more than two years, stay married, or achieve their goals.

Our *deen* seeks to train us to live by this principle. For example, we wake up before sunrise to pray *fajr*. Some parents may think that allowing their children to study for an exam until late at night is the right thing to do even though their children may miss praying *fajr* on time as a result, when in reality, they have only brought about ruin. Nothing brings greater success than being able to strengthen one's resolve and practise patience, for the correct translation of the word *sabr* is the ability to delay reward.

The Love for a Lost Son

Nuh (a.s.)

One of the most difficult family situations is when righteousness is sought by some but there is a renegade amongst the relatives, like in the example of Nuh (a.s.). He was a great prophet of Allah who called his people to righteousness for 950 years. Nuh (a.s.) did not live through just a single generation—Allah (s.w.t.) extended his life that generations would die off but he would remain. He spoke to men and women, and their children, and their children's children, and so on. Nuh (a.s.) was consistently calling people to Allah (s.w.t.). However, his people rebelled and turned their back to the truth, including his own flesh and blood. So we can understand his *du'a* and where it was coming from when he prayed to Allah (s.w.t.), *I called these people day and night and I found nothing in my call to them, except that they would turn away from You.*

His own son, whom he raised and taught how to walk and talk, whom he held and played with, and whom he loved and nurtured upon faith, chose not to submit to Allah (s.w.t.). Imagine the plight of an *imam*—let alone a prophet or a messenger with divine order from Allah (s.w.t.)—who stood before a congregation of people advising them of righteousness and condemning sinfulness, but they turn to him saying, *You call to us when your own son stands before you and rejects you?*

Day after day, Nuh (a.s.) called out to his son. *Come to the mercy of Allah!* His son turned away time and again.

Until the order of Allah had come to pass, Nuh (a.s.) made a *du'a* against his people. Allah (s.w.t.) answered the *du'a* eventually, but Nuh (a.s.) wished for one assurance from Allah (s.w.t.).

He said, *O Allah, save me and my family.*

Allah (s.w.t.) then made a promise, *I will save you and your family.*

With that hope, the rain began to fall. The earth fractured, and its springs began to overwhelm. The dams began to break. People began to drown.

Nuh called on to his son, who was trying to find protection from the rising waters. *O my dearest son, although you have rebelled, I will never give up on you. My hand will always be outstretched for you, although you have disgraced me and other people have turned away on account of your rejection of me. My son, of all the years that you have rebelled against Allah, I stand with my hand reaching out to you. Come aboard the ship if you can come to faith.*

Here is an important matter to understand. As part of our faith, we can never make the illegitimate legitimate. We love our children, but we will never accept them without faith. It is the command of Allah that none will be saved except the one who has accepted the religion. Although we would give up our lives for our children, we cannot give up our faith for our children. *My blood flows within you, but my iman is a greater bond.*

His son threw it back in his face. At times, we learn the lesson the hard way, that no matter how much love, compassion, and forgiveness we give, some people in our lives will still refuse to accept the faith—there will always be those who will turn away. Even Prophet Muhammad (s.a.w.) had those whom he loved so dearly who would not accept his call.

The Prophet (s.a.w.) would sit with his uncle, Abu Talib, in his final hours. *Just give me the words: "La ilaha illAllah"*, he said earnestly. *I will defend you before Allah if you give me these words.* But it was not meant to be uttered. Even though the love of the Prophet (s.a.w.) was complete, it was insufficient to turn Abu Talib's heart to faith. It was the *qadr* of Allah.

Similarly, Nuh (a.s.) loved his son. *My son, come aboard. I cannot change what is wrong to be what is right. I cannot accept you just as you want to accept yourself. I can only accept you in the way that Allah seeks you. If I am seeking you the way Allah wants, that is where I can allow you access.*

Yet, his son went further in arrogance.

Allah (s.w.t.) warns us of this in the Qur'an. There are people who, when it is said to them, *Fear your Lord—humble yourselves to Allah*, will only increase in their arrogance.

The son of Nuh (a.s.) said, *My father, I do not need you and your Lord. I will climb that mountain. I am fit, able, healthy, and strong. I can do and make decisions for myself.*

Nuh (a.s.) said to his son, *My son, none will find salvation today, except by the mercy of Allah. It is not your strength; it is your heart. It is not your ability; it is your faith. It is the rahmah of Allah that you should seek, not just protection from the water. My son, you are shortsighted; you are thinking of the dunya when you should be concerned with the akhirah.*

Allah (s.w.t.) then sent a crashing wave that pulled the disbelieving son under the water, drowning him.

It was not that Nuh (a.s.) had any distrust in Allah (s.w.t.), but he wanted to find affirmation. Thus, he called out to Allah (s.w.t.), *My Lord, when you make a promise, it is kept. My Lord, you promised to save me and my family. And that son is from me; he is from my family. You ordered that your promise would always be kept. He is from my family, but he drowned. O Allah, I had the hope in my du'a, in my love for my boy that You would turn his heart to faith. O Allah, I made du'a after du'a, and I called and I invoked, but he drowned. Is it that You did not keep your promise to me, O Allah?"*

Allah (s.w.t.) responded to Nuh (a.s.), *You must come to understand that when a person has chosen a path of wickedness, blood no longer matters. He is no longer your family if he has chosen a family of crime, a family of sin, a family of wicked deeds. That became to him more important than what you call him to. Do not ask Me what you have no knowledge of.*

Nuh (a.s.) understood. This became another powerful lesson of love—the love of Allah and clearing our hearts of any doubts between ourselves and Him.

The Lessons

1st *Lesson*

Never give up on anyone. Even if they are caught up in the middle of a raging river of *fitnah*, in the middle of their addiction, or in the middle of their sin, your hand must always be outstretched to help them out of it if they wish to grab it.

No one should have to fear that if they were to knock on their parents' door to say some very tough words, they would be turned away. Some young people might say to their parents upon leaving a path of sin, *I have made tawbah to Allah; please let me in.* Yet, some parents would still reject them.

How dare we close the door that Allah (s.w.t.) has kept open? How can we be blind to the example of the prophets? It does not matter how much pain has been caused. It becomes difficult to love those whom we feel are unworthy, but that is where we find the love of Allah. It is finding it in those who have disappointed you and even Allah (s.w.t.). Be the one who invites to the path that returns them to Allah (s.w.t.).

2nd Lesson

Although we may love, the *qadr* may be different. No matter how near we are to Allah (s.w.t.) or how faithful we are to Allah (s.w.t.), we cannot ever assume that what we want in life and every *du'a* we make will be granted by Him.

Thus, Allah (s.w.t.) said to Nuh (a.s.) *Do not ask Me what you have no knowledge of. Perhaps, if I were to answer with what you wanted and your son were to come onto the ship, it would cause a greater fitnah to you than for you to have lost him now.*

3rd Lesson

Even for the prophets of Allah, there were heartaches and difficulties in their family. Do not look at your home to find dysfunction in it and say, *O Allah, what have I done to deserve this?* Nuh (a.s.) had done nothing to deserve the loss of his son in rebellion against Allah (s.w.t.). Do not look at somebody else and say, *They must have committed a sin for their son to be this way.* Do not ever look at anyone with contempt if Allah (s.w.t.) has saved you.

Remember the words of Imam Ibn Al-Qayyim where he said, *When you see someone in difficulty who is unable to change for themselves in something haram that has happened in their home, look to them with the eyes of qadr. Look to them with an eye that sees fate as having been averted from you and affected them. Perhaps in their eyes, there may be something they will see the fate in you that you have not seen yet yourself.*

We must never think that our knowledge is greater than the knowledge of Allah because we do not know more than what Allah (s.w.t.) knows.

Love: True or False
Qabil & Habil

Allah (s.w.t.) mentions in Qur'an,

۞ وَٱتْلُ عَلَيْهِمْ نَبَأَ ٱبْنَىْ ءَادَمَ بِٱلْحَقِّ
إِذْ قَرَّبَا قُرْبَانًا فَتُقُبِّلَ مِنْ أَحَدِهِمَا وَلَمْ
يُتَقَبَّلْ مِنَ ٱلْـَٔاخَرِ قَالَ لَأَقْتُلَنَّكَ ۖ قَالَ
إِنَّمَا يَتَقَبَّلُ ٱللَّهُ مِنَ ٱلْمُتَّقِينَ ﴿٢٧﴾

And recite to them the story of Adam's two sons, in truth, when they both offered a sacrifice [to Allah], and it was accepted from one of them but was not accepted from the other. Said [the latter], "I will surely kill you." Said [the former], "Indeed, Allah only accepts from the righteous [who fear Him]."
(Surah Al-Ma'idah, 5:27)

Adam (a.s.) wanted the *nikah* (marriage ceremony) of his two sons to be performed with two different women. One of them coveted the future wife of the other, so he said, *No, I want her.* Adam (a.s.) said that the decision will be made by Allah (s.w.t.); the two of them would make an offering, and whoever Allah (s.w.t.) accepted from, he would be the man to marry her.

At that time, Allah (s.w.t.) would send fire from the heavens to consume what had been offered. Allah (s.w.t.) accepted the offering of one and not the other. The heart impassioned with sinful love could not accept what Allah (s.w.t.) had decreed. Out of rage, he killed his brother.

The root cause of the very first murder committed in human history was a sinful, impassioned love. *SubhanAllah*. That wayward glance, that desire that is not kept, that seeking of what Allah (s.w.t.) has forbidden—all that resulted not just in sin but also in the greatest crime. The Prophet (s.a.w.) said no human being is ever murdered except a part of the sin of that murder is added to the record of the very first one to institute the concept of killing amongst humanity, the first son of Adam (a.s.). He had murdered his own brother because of the desire that came from shallow lust.

Thereafter, he son of Adam sat in distraught, not knowing what to do—until then, no one had died and there had never been any funeral. Allah (s.w.t.) sent a crow to show him how to bury the dead. The crow began to dig the earth with its beak, claw, and foot until it made a hole in the ground. Then, it buried something in the hole, in front of him. Having watched the crow, it dawned upon him that he should do the same. He buried the body of his brother, and he became among the remorseful.

The Lessons

1st Lesson

Here is a very important lesson about love. True love is that which is pleasing to Allah (s.w.t.). Sinful love is referred to by the *'ulama* as *ishq*: it looks like love, but to achieve it, you have to disobey Allah (s.w.t.). It is where you text someone without your family's knowledge. It is where you meet up without people seeing you. It is that sinful love where you make an arrangement that if people were to see you, it would be humiliating and upsetting for you and those whom you love. It feels like love, but it is expressed for a reason and in a way that is not valuing you but consuming you instead.

How many of us love eating the meat of a chicken? Do we love chicken enough to take it and slit its throat? And broil it? And barbecue it? Is it that we love the chicken or we love what chicken does for us?

Therefore, when you use that word, "love", consider what you mean by it. Are you a commodity that is loved for what you provide or for who you are? If a person says, *I love you*, are they saying, *I love you*, or are they saying, *I love what I do with you, what I hear from you, or what I received from you*?

Allah (s.w.t.) says to us in the Qur'an,

زُيِّنَ لِلنَّاسِ حُبُّ ٱلشَّهَوَٰتِ مِنَ
ٱلنِّسَآءِ وَٱلْبَنِينَ ...

Beautified for people is the love of that which they desire: of women, children...
(Surah Ali 'Imran, 3:14)

It has been made for men in particular, but also for humanity in general, that they love to fulfil what they desire from women. It is not that he loves you; rather, he loves what you do for him. It is not that she loves you; rather, she loves what you do for her.

That is not the love of the Qur'an. That is not the love of the Prophet (s.a.w.). That is not the love that we have described. The true love that we have described is the love of sacrifice and giving, not of taking or consuming what is not our own.

Therefore, if we think of the love we give to anyone we find ourselves in a relationship with, even our children or our own parents, is it a love of consumption or provision? *Do I love my son only when he is obedient to me? If this love is conditional, if he turns away from me, will I abandon him?* If we think of the love we have for our spouses, is it a love commitment between two individuals, two hearts, two souls, like that of the Prophet (s.a.w.) and those whom he loves? Or is it only because of one's status?

When we seek love through sin, it can never be achieved. That becomes an important lesson. The reality is that Allah (s.w.t.) seeks for us a path of purity. The best way to ensure longevity and a love that is not of consumption but of giving and pleasing to Allah (s.w.t.) is to adhere to the *shari'ah*—the path that leads us to the water of life and to the place of success.

2nd Lesson

Many people misunderstand the *hadith* of the Prophet (s.a.w.) about the criteria when choosing someone for marriage: beauty, wealth, lineage, and religious commitment. The Prophet (s.a.w.) was not recommending us to judge a person based on this order; he was telling us to weigh them out. Is the beauty of the woman one is marrying sufficient for him, or is it too much? *SubhanAllah*, a man may look like Shrek, yet he asks for a Cinderella. He may be unemployed, yet he seeks to marry an aristocrat, thinking that it is sufficient to provide her with a bus pass when her family has given her a key to her own car.

The Prophet (s.a.w.) was telling us that when the time for marriage comes, we need to give it some thought. Imam As-Shafi'i spoke about the capacity of equity between the man and the woman. Is there something measurable between the two of them of an equitable state, in terms of beauty, age, status, or wealth? You do not marry a rich woman because she is going to make you rich.

SubhanAllah, in the Sunnah, a woman can give *zakat* (tithe) to her husband, but a man cannot give *zakat* to his wife. What is yours is hers, and what is hers is hers.

Once, a woman came to the Prophet (s.a.w.) and said, *O Messenger of Allah, the husband that I had has found a financial downturn. We had equitable means, but now I want to help out. Can I give my husband zakat?*

The Prophet replied, *Yes.*

Your wife does not give you money for you; it is *zakat*; it is *sadaqah* (charity). *Allahu akbar!* So when one gets married, the woman's beauty and wealth count. Can the spouses sustain themselves on what they are choosing? In our *shari'ah* (Islamic law), all four *madhahib* (schools of thought) say that if one cannot establish what was once agreed prior to the *nikah,* the wife no longer has to stay in her husband's home or obey him. If it is requested, separation will be granted, because the husband forfeited what was a miscalculation, that is, she was not the right person. But if she wishes to give him *zakat* and *sadaqah* before Allah (s.w.t.), she is giving her wealth not for paying the bills, but it is a loan for the husband to return and spend on her. So before marriage, think of the four.

3rd Lesson

Many of us are disconnected from the Qur'an and the seemingly separate sciences of the world that we are living in today. There is the science of anthropology. There is the science of sociology. There is the science of biology and evolution. At times, it can be difficult to connect the Qur'an with them.

When we look back at human history, sometimes, we assume that the knowledge Allah (s.w.t.) gave Adam (a.s.) was inherited by all of his children. In reality, his children did not know what Adam knew. Human beings are taught by Allah (s.w.t.) by the study of the pen, and we have to evolve in our learning and knowledge.

One of the first principles of anthropology is that humans mimic animals. In the Qur'anic story of the first death in the history of mankind, Allah (s.w.t.) showed the son of Adam how to bury the dead—not through a revelation brought by Jibril (a.s.), but from the example of an animal, a crow.

SubhanAllah, it is an element of science that we have within the Qur'an, not found in biblical narratives or anywhere else. This is a beautiful symmetry where Allah (s.w.t.) gives us evidence of things that we have come to unravel in our life story today.

The Love of a Husband & Wife
Ibrahim (a.s.) & Sarah

Ibrahim (a.s.) and his beautiful wife Sarah were rejected from the land where he gained his prominence of seeking to teach people *tawhid.* As they wandered the earth, they came to an unknown city.

The king of that city was an oppressive tyrant who subjugated those residing in his kingdom. If a man was married to a woman, for the king to establish his authority, the king would know the man's wife carnally for that man to be given access to cross or to reside in his land.

This was not unusual. Even the British Empire used to have this concept of a landowner being given the right to live there and to govern the people by the King of England, and even in Scotland and Ireland, if a man and woman got married, the landlord or the mayor of the town would know the man's wife first before he himself entered upon her. This was meant to instil fear in them, and the practice still exists to this day in certain communities. When we hear of 15,000 births as a result of the systematic rape of our Rohingya Muslim women, we see that sexual violence has always been used as a method of subjugation.

Allah (s.w.t.) speaks of this in the story of Ibrahim (a.s.) and Sarah. They were both brought in front of the court and the king.

Who is she to you? the king demanded.

In Surah Maryam, verse 41, Allah (s.w.t.) mentions Ibrahim as "a man of truth and a prophet". But at that moment, out of love and sacrifice for his wife, he looked the king in the face and lied.

This is my sister, he said.

With that lie, he saved the honour of his wife, and they exited the land untouched.

However, Ibrahim (a.s.) did not forgive himself for this. In *Sahih Al-Bukhari*, Abi Sa'id Al-Khudri (r.a.) narrated from the Prophet (s.a.w.) that on the Day of Judgement, when we come to Prophet Ibrahim (a.s.) asking him to save us on that day, he will say, *Go to someone else. I lied in my life three times. I am scared for myself. So go to someone else.*

He held it in his heart until the Day of Judgement that he had lied. On that day, he will fear Allah's judgement, even though the lie was for the salvation and protection of his beloved wife, Sarah.

When we remember the example of the love Ibrahim (a.s.) for his wife, fulfiling his duties as the guardian of his family, it is clear that he did what he had to do in order to protect his wife, even if it meant holding himself accountable before Allah (s.w.t.).

The Lesson

Allah (s.w.t.) has given men something called *qawwamah*. He says in the Qur'an,

ٱلرِّجَالُ قَوَّٰمُونَ عَلَى ٱلنِّسَآءِ بِمَا فَضَّلَ ٱللَّهُ بَعۡضَهُمۡ عَلَىٰ بَعۡضٖ وَبِمَآ أَنفَقُواْ مِنۡ أَمۡوَٰلِهِمۡۚ

Men are in charge of women by [right of] what Allah has given one over the other and what they spend [for maintenance] from their wealth...
(Surah An-Nisa', 4:34)

The words "*qawwamun 'ala an-nisa'*" are meant to be established in service to the wives. The concept of being *qawwam* is to be vigilant.

One of the greatest examples of being *qawwam* is Musa (a.s.). Allah (s.w.t.) said to him, as he stood in the Mount Tur in Sina in his first communion with Allah (s.w.t.), *Musa, what is in your hand?*

He replied, *It is my staff. I lean on it.*

The ʻ*ulama* of *tafsir* said Musa (a.s.) leaned on it in three ways that showed how he was a man of *qawwam. I lean on the stick to prevent injury because I have a wife and children that I must look after. I lean on the stick so that when I am injured, I do not sit down and then ask women to do the work for me. I lean on the stick so that even when I am injured, I will hobble and I will not rest because I have a responsibility behind me. I lean on the stick so that when I am exhausted, I would rather put my hand on it, even though I am asleep, and I remain vigilant so that people from a distance will see me and not come near for there is someone on guard.*

What does it mean to be responsible for one's wife and to love her?

Let's take the example of Adam (a.s.). Allah (s.w.t.) describes to us their story in the Qur'an,

فَأَكَلَا مِنْهَا فَبَدَتْ لَهُمَا سَوْءَٰتُهُمَا وَطَفِقَا يَخْصِفَانِ عَلَيْهِمَا مِن وَرَقِ ٱلْجَنَّةِ ۚ وَعَصَىٰٓ ءَادَمُ رَبَّهُۥ فَغَوَىٰ ﴿١٢١﴾

So they both ate from the tree and then their nakedness was exposed to them, prompting them to cover themselves with leaves from

Paradise. So Adam disobeyed his Lord, and [so] lost his way.
(Surah Taha, 20:121)

Allah (s.w.t.) uses the language of duality in the first part of this verse: both Adam (a.s.) and his wife were there, and both of them ate from the prohibited tree at the same time. Nevertheless, when Allah (s.w.t.) speaks about who had erred, He only mentions Adam's name. The man is the one who is meant to be on guard, standing to attention. Ultimately, he is the one responsible for the direction that he leads his family and his household in.

To love as a husband is that you give something without expecting to receive anything. When you look at the examples of Prophet Muhammad (s.a.w.) and how he expressed his love to his wives, it is always about what he gave and not what he received.

The Love for the Ummah
Zakariyya (a.s.)

In the final years of his life, Zakariyya (a.s.) looked at himself—his hair has grown white and ashen, his bone has become weak—and he turned to Allah (s.w.t.) in a *du'a* that he has been repeating years after years. *O my Lord, I seek from you a child—a blessed child—who will inherit from me and from the family of Ya'qub prophethood.*

Where is the love in this story?

Zakariyya (a.s.) knew that they were at the turning point in human history: Bani Isra'il had turned to wickedness and went astray from Allah (s.w.t.). And he knew that if his life would come to an end, there would be no prophet left among Bani Isra'il to guide them towards Allah (s.w.t.). Zakariyya (a.s.) was concerned.

What do we need? he thought.

O Allah, give me a son. I might not be around for long to raise him, but he is going to lead my ummah. I want him to lead after I am gone.

He asked that Allah (s.w.t.) bless him with a son—not for himself, but for his people. A son who would carry the future of the *deen*, one who would be as concerned about the *ummah* as he was. Zakariyya (a.s.) yearned for a son not out of his own want, but he wished for his people to have a leader after his passing. That was the hope of Zakariyya (a.s.).

However, Allah (s.w.t.) had decreed that Bani Isra'il would soon no longer carry the prophethood; a chosen one from among Bani Isma'il would become the seal of the prophets—Muhammad (s.a.w.). But Allah (s.w.t.) answered the *du'a* of Zakariyya (a.s.) and granted him a son named Yahya.

Zakariyya (a.s.) was elated. He was going to have a son—even though he was extremely old and his wife was barren—a righteous son who would become a prophet of his people and continue the mission after him. Yet, Yahya (a.s.) was martyred, young in age, before his father. In a *hadith* recorded by Imam Ahmad, the Prophet (s.a.w.) said that Yahya (a.s.) was a martyr, the son of a martyr, because after Yahya (a.s.) was murdered, a mob filled with grudge and hostility pursued and ultimately murdered his father, Zakariyya (a.s.), as well.

According to some scholars, the name "Yahya" comes from the word "*hayy*", meaning life. But Yahya (a.s.) only lived a short life in the *dunya*. He was destined to be martyred and to live with Allah (s.w.t.) in the afterlife in the way that Allah (s.w.t.) seeks of the martyrs. Allah (s.w.t.) says in the Qur'an,

وَلَا تَحْسَبَنَّ ٱلَّذِينَ قُتِلُوا۟ فِى سَبِيلِ

ٱللَّهِ أَمۡوَٰتَۢاۚ بَلۡ أَحۡيَآءٌ عِندَ رَبِّهِمۡ يُرۡزَقُونَ ١٦٩

And never think of those who have been killed in the cause of Allah as dead. Rather, they are alive with their Lord, receiving provision.
(Surah Ali 'Imran, 3:169)

The Lessons

1st Lesson

The expectation we have of our children should not be based on our personal needs or wants; it should extend beyond to benefit the future of the Muslim *ummah*. We may need our children to continue the family business, or we may want them to become a doctor because it is a respected profession with a good income, *alhamdulillah*—but perhaps there is a missing void in our community that our children may be able to fill with their talents.

There are many examples among the great *imams* we have today whose initial vocation was not the *deen*; they studied engineering, pharmacy, geology, business, and so on. Yet they chose to commit to the study of the religion and became a teacher or an *imam* out of passion.

When you recognise a talent in someone, look through the eyes of Zakariyya (a.s.), and you will see a special kind of love, not for yourself and your own family, but for the needs and the prospects of the whole *ummah*. It is about thinking 15, 20 years ahead and having a vision for the future.

2nd Lesson

Yahya (a.s.) became that martyr who was set as an example for our *ummah*. We may have hopes for our children and their future, but sometimes, things do not go as planned. It is a fact of life that we have to accept. But know that we will be rewarded for our intentions and the targets that we seek to meet.

Do not limit our concerns and efforts to just ourselves and our families; have this farsightedness to look beyond our small existence to serve a much larger purpose in the community and for humanity. Loving is not holding; loving is giving for the sake of Allah (s.w.t.).

Birr

We always hear of this statement about *birr* in the Qur'an, where Allah (s.w.t.) says,

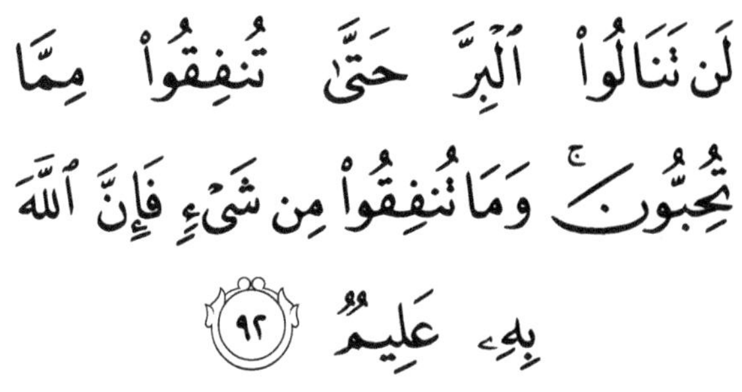

Never will you attain the good [reward] until you spend [in the way of Allah] from that which you love. And whatever you spend—indeed, Allah is Knowing of it.
(Surah Ali 'Imran, 3:92)

What does the word *birr* mean linguistically? *Birr* is something that is barren but produces fruits. Imagine yourself in a scorching desert, with no rain, no water, no irrigation; but in the middle of that desert, there is a beautiful rose garden. You wonder—*how does this garden sustain itself? How, in this desolate place, can this good thing exists?* This is what is called *birr*.

It is the opposite of what is natural. It is the opposite of human emotion, which is inclined to hold on to rather than part with something, especially things that we love the most. Time, energy, family, wealth—to give these away would leave one in the state of barrenness from the perspective of the *dunya*.

If we study the words of Allah in the Qur'an, one of the echoing themes we will find is *birrul walidayn*, kindness to the parents. The reality of what we see in our family relationship is the opposite of *birr*.

Birr goes beyond what is natural. It is that you become not the desert but the gardens and the vegetations in the desert. You become like the rain that has brought the earth to growth when nothing else could grow it. You become the one who changes the hearts of two people who have separated—you connect them together. You become the one who, by the blessing of Allah, have righteousness. What is this righteousness? You make what others considered impossible possible—because of your love and your willingness to give.

All of the love stories in the Qur'an have the connotations of *birr*: protection, *qawwam*, endearment, sacrifice, acceptance, allowing redemption and return after sin, opening what others closed and uplifting those who others pushed down. They are the opposite of what is conventional, the oxymoron of the sinfulness that others display, and the righteous rain of *barakah* into the heart and mind of those who are distant from Allah (s.w.t.).

CPSIA information can be obtained
at www.ICGtesting.com
Printed in the USA
LVHW050054040323
740881LV00012B/926